RELEASING KINGS AND QUEENS INTO GOD'S ORIGINAL INTENT

KINGDOM SECRETS TO RESTORING NATIONS BACK TO GOD

ABRAHAM JOHN

Releasing Kings and Queens into God's Original Intent
Kingdom Secrets to Restoring Nations Back to God

Copyright © 2016 by Abraham John

Published by Abraham John
Maximum Impact Ministries

www.maximpact.org
email: mim@maximpact.org
(720) 420 9873

ISBN: 978-1-948330-17-6

All rights reserved. No part of this book may be reproduced or transmitted in any form or by any means, electronic or mechanical—including photocopying, recording, or by any information storage and retrieval system without permission in writing from the author. Please direct your inquiries to mim@maximpact.org. All emphasis or additions within Scripture quotations are the author's own.

Unless otherwise indicated, all Scripture quotations are taken from the *New King James Version* of the Holy Bible. Copyright ©1995-2010, The Zondervan Corporation. All Rights Reserved.

Scripture quotations marked (KJV) are from the *King James Version* of the Holy Bible Electronic Database. Copyright © 1995-2010, The Zondervan Corporation. All Rights Reserved.

CONTENTS

Introduction		5
Chapter 1:	How it All Began	11
Chapter 2:	The Real Beginning	27
Chapter 3:	The Fall of Lucifer	47
Chapter 4:	God and Jesus—as Kings	63
Chapter 5:	Believers as Kings and Queens	73
Chapter 6:	The Responsibilities of a King	89
Chapter 7:	The Character and Nature of a King	107
More Books & Resources		119

INTRODUCTION

As a believer in Christ, you have more than one identity in the spirit. In the natural realm you have more than one form of official identification document (ID).

IDs are required to prove who you are and what you can do in your country. If you are driving and a police officer stops you, you have to show your driver's license to prove that you have the right to drive. You don't show him your passport, and if you do, though it might be a valid form of ID, it's not the correct one for that situation.

When you want to travel to another country and you are at the border or at an airport, you are required to have a passport. You would not show your driver's license. In order to prove your nationality and place of birth you need a birth certificate.

These are all various forms of ID intended for different purposes.

It is important to keep your IDs safe and secure. If your ID is lost or stolen, you will not be able to show it when it is required, and you will not enjoy the privileges permitted by your government without it.

For example, a passport is required to cross most borders. If you are at the border and you forgot to bring your passport, the immigration authorities will deny you the privilege of crossing the border and entering their country.

It doesn't matter how much you argue or cry, they will not let you in, simply because you did not present the required form of ID. It is the same in the spirit.

You may have been a Christian for a long time, but if you do not realize and use the right form of identity, you may not receive and enjoy everything God has prepared for you.

In the natural realm, everything connected to your life works around having and presenting different forms of ID timeously and appropriately.

Every valid transaction and official dealing requires an appropriate ID. If you cannot provide a valid, ID that transaction will be declined or delayed until you can provide one.

Many of our spiritual transactions have been dormant or on-hold because we failed to recognize and assert who we are in the spirit.

God has given us different forms of identity in the spirit, each serving a different purpose. For so long we have been teaching people about only one form of spiritual identity —which is being a child of God, but that is not the only form of ID available to believers.

It is like having your birth certificate, which, as you know, is not enough to do everything you were born to do in your country. It is the most foundational ID that gives you the right to verify or obtain other forms of ID. Just having a birth certificate does not give you all the rights to accomplish everything you are called to do.

A birth certificate is one of the first IDs a person will receive in life that proves your citizenship and nationality. In the spiritual realm, it is the same.

When you are Born Again you become a citizen of a different country—the kingdom of heaven.

INTRODUCTION

As you know, a kingdom is always ruled by a king. In God's kingdom, He is the King; and when you are Born Again, you became His son or daughter. That is the identity that we are all familiar with. Sons and daughters of a king are princes and princesses.

However, in God's kingdom, you were never naturally born as a prince or princess. Rather, He gives you a free upgrade as a king and a queen the moment you are Born Again into His kingdom.

When Jesus was born He was not born as a prince. He was born as a King (Matthew 2:2; John 18:37). However, for you as a believer, that is your second spiritual identity.

If you are a man, you are a king; and if you are a woman, you are a queen on this earth *right now*. Though queens are not specified, it is nevertheless implicit, as it logically understood that if there are *kings* there are *queens* as well. This is very important to understand. The enemy will always try to challenge or steal your identity.

When Jesus was on this earth, the enemy challenged His identity as the Son of God. Satan told Him, "If you are the Son of God… (Matthew 4:3b). Then, when He was brought for trial, Pilot challenged his identity as a king. He asked, "Are you the King of the Jews?" or "Are you a king then?" (John 18:33b; 37a). While He answered Pilot, He never tried to prove Himself to Satan in the wilderness.

Jesus did not have a palace and servants like earthly kings do, but, rather, He was a king in every other significant sense of the word. When God reveals your ID in His kingdom as His king, you may not have all the natural things to prove who you are. You need to grow into it. Initially, in the kingdom of God we all begin with a revelation.

If you are saved, the Bible says you have a calling (2 Timothy 1:9). Your calling is your third form of ID in the spiritual sense.

If you work in a company, they will issue you a company ID that gives you access to their building, to open the doors, and enter into your place of work. You do not bring your birth certificate to work every day. You need a different form of ID to enter your workplace—an ID that is authorized by the company.

When the sons of Sceva tried to cast out demons, those demons questioned the their' identity. They said, "Jesus I know, and Paul I know; but who are you?" (Acts 19:14-16). Sceva's sons did not have the right form of ID in the spirit, so they could not cast out those demons.

Your calling gives you another form of ID in the spirit, and it gives you authority to do certain things in the spirit-world.

In the kingdom of God, your sonship gives you access to heaven and to the throne room of God. That's your relationship with your heavenly Father. Being kings and queens gives you the right to do certain things on earth on behalf of your Father's kingdom. That's your *position* on this earth.

Your calling determines your jurisdiction; that is, what you can and cannot do, and where you can do it on this earth. That's your *assignment* on this earth.

We know the whole creation is waiting for the revealing of the sons of God. God manifests through each of His sons and daughters differently. Jesus is the Son of God, but He manifested as the Savior and Redeemer of this world. Adam was a son of God, and his assignment was to till and keep the garden. Thus, God manifests differently through each of us to restore or set free a part of creation.

God used more people in the Bible in government positions or to influence governments than any other area of society. This is because a government has so much influence on a nation and its people.

INTRODUCTION

There are more kings than prophets or any other ministry gifts recorded in the Bible. He has such an interest in government because He Himself is a King and has a kingdom.

In the Old Testament there were mainly three offices: *kings, prophets*, and *priests*.

When God decided to restore or build a nation, He raised up a king. When He wanted to restore a people back to Himself, He raised up a prophet. When He wanted to restore or revive the spiritual life of people He would raise up a priest.

The reason why nations are deteriorating is not because there are not enough prophets and *priests,* but because there are not enough *kings*. When kings are released into their kingly office and God's original intent, nations will be restored to God.

In the New Testament Jesus has made us kings and priests to our God and Father (Revelation 1:6; 5:10). Every believer is a king and a priest, not some kings and others priests. Kings live in a kingdom. By its very definition, the word *king* means someone who rules or holds a place of influence.

Man was designed and created by God to build and to live in a kingdom. It is up to us whether we build our own little kingdoms, the devil's kingdom, or the kingdom of God.

In every man is the desire to design, govern, rule, build, establish, raise up, and accomplish something, or to help someone else do it. When a man cannot do that, he gets frustrated.

If a man does not have that desire in him, something happened to his *manhood* and it needs to be restored. Similarly, a woman was designed and created to help a man who builds a kingdom; thus, to be the queen by his side. If a woman does not have that desire, then something happened to her *womanhood* and it needs to be restored. It is their natural instinct.

An erroneous teaching came into the body of Christ in the 1990s that taught that kings are those involved in business or making money, and priests are those in ministry. As a result, we almost lost our nation. Covetousness and greed took hold of many mighty men, and the enemy destroyed their lives.

As a tragic result, those who are called to be kings and queens either left the church, or now sit in the pews—frustrated and angry because of what is going down in their nation.

They do not know what to do because they were never taught properly about it. Sadly, all they have to talk about now, is how their favorite sports team is doing. This book is intended to release those kings and queens to rediscover God's original intent for them.

My prayer is that the Lord will use this book to bring clarity and direction to those mighty men and women whom the Lord wants to use to rebuild the broken walls of this nation; to bring prayer back to our schools, to train our children in the ways of the Lord, and to love God and their family and nation more than they love the things of this world.

Chapter 1
HOW IT ALL BEGAN

A long, long, very long time ago on a far-away planet, lived a great King. This was a King like no other. He was the wisest and richest King that has ever lived.

One special thing about this King, is that whatever He spoke, came into existence. There was no one to compare to Him in power, wealth, and glory. There was no king like Him before nor will there be after Him. His kingdom was the most prosperous and glorious.

Whoever loved and honored this King was rewarded with great riches and blessings of every kind. And whoever did not honor or obey Him was cursed and finally, removed from His kingdom.

However, He was also very kind, merciful, and ready to forgive any wrong that anyone did against him or against one of His citizens. Though He was perfect in all His ways, most people misunderstood His intentions.

Innumerable servants served Him day and night. When I say *innumerable*, I mean that literally there was no way to count the number of His servants. He needed that many, because the many things He accomplished in His kingdom and the things He oversaw or ruled were unlimited.

Hence, His servants were appointed into different ranks. There was one rank that just sang His praises, day and night. They composed songs about His greatness, holiness, and wisdom.

Then, there was another group that bore and took His messages to whoever He wanted to communicate.

Thus, each dimension of His kingdom was managed by different ranks of servants. They not only looked different in form, but revealed a different sphere of His glory and facets of His character.

Even though this kingdom existed from a very long time ago, this was the most advanced kingdom in every way possible. The technology was incomparable.

The King knew the very thoughts of all His kingdom subjects at all times. His messengers traveled faster than the speed of light.

Despite today's advancements and cutting-edge developments mankind boasts about, even way back then, no one could come up with ideas or technology anywhere close to what He had in His kingdom.

No one could challenge this King. His counsel and wisdom were unsearchable.

The King's many close associates working and serving Him were in charge of managing and developing His great wealth, businesses, and trade. Of all the close associates He had, there was one in particular who was closer to Him than all others. He knew the King and His ways more than any other at that time. He was known as the Light Bearer.

This close associate was in charge of the King's wealth, businesses, manufacturing, trade, developments, innovation, and even the making of music in His kingdom.

CHAPTER 1 | HOW IT ALL BEGAN

The king was very pleased with this associate and he was very trusted. Everyone in the kingdom came to know of this associate and his splendor, wisdom, capabilities, and accomplishments.

Know that if such a great King was to entrust all His wealth, wisdom, and the trade of His kingdom to anyone else, that associate must be very special. Thus, everyone respected him because of that.

As with every king, it is in their nature to honor and bless those who are faithful and close to them. Also, it is in every king to constantly look for opportunities to expand their territory into new spheres of influence.

One day the King called all of His close associates together for a very important meeting. They did not meet like that very often. So, they all knew in their hearts that whatever the King was going to tell them was very important; or He would not have called such a meeting in the first place. Each time He did so, something very special always took place.

The King began to tell them about His kingdom and its glory— how much it had grown and expanded and continued to grow every moment. He appreciated all of their efforts, commitment, and hard work. He said, "I have no intention of slowing down. I want My kingdom to continue to grow and expand, and I will do anything and everything to make that happen."

Then He turned to His closest associate, the Light Bearer, and acclaimed all he had accomplished; honoring him in the presence of everyone.

Then the King announced something very important to all the assembled associates. He said, "I have decided to promote one of My close associates today."

Everyone gasped and held their breaths because none of them knew who it was going to be. Each one wondered and waited to see who had been chosen.

The King continued, "He has been serving Me faithfully for eons. And now, the time has come for me to release him into this new responsibility in My kingdom. The way I am promoting this associate is like never before. I am creating a new territory for my kingdom in a far-away dimension. This territory must exactly represent everything in my kingdom. Everything in this new territory will be done exactly as we do things here in My kingdom. And to manage that new territory I am going to appoint one of you. He will rule as a king over this territory; he can set up his own throne and will have servants, and will be in charge of My *Will* being done there as it is here.

I am appointing my close associate, the Light Bearer, to be the king of this new territory because no one is wiser or more creative than he is."

Although everyone else was understandably somewhat taken aback because they were not chosen, they clapped their hands and shouted with joy. Notwithstanding, they all approved of the King's decision. No one could counsel Him otherwise nor challenge His decision.

The King continued, saying, "Not only am I appointing My Light Bearer to manage this new territory for Me, I am sending many of My servants to assist him in making this new sphere just like My kingdom here at home. I know it is going to be a huge task, so I am releasing everything he needs from my kingdom to make this new territory just like Mine here."

Without pausing, He announced, "I am going to call this new territory *Terra* because the materials and substance in this new territory are different from what I have here."

So, the King spoke, and it was done as He spoke—the Light Bearer and many thousands of the King's servants were seconded to this new territory in a moment of time.

The Light Bearer was naturally both very happy and excited. He had been waiting for such an opportunity for a long time. He was

CHAPTER 1 | HOW IT ALL BEGAN

perfect in his wisdom and imagined that he could create almost anything he wanted.

Having been put in charge over all the King's wealth, for example, he had a very special robe that he wore. This robe was made of very special and precious stones and metals—sardius, topaz, diamond, beryl, onyx, jasper, sapphire, turquoise, emerald—were just some of these.

Depending on what he did at any given moment, the robe kept changing in color and the type of stones it was made of. It was the most magnificent robe anyone ever possessed in the King's kingdom.

It is the custom of kings to be arrayed in costly robes, as those so honored in the kingdom.

As the Light Bearer was very special to the King, that He created this special robe for him because of all the majestic titles he bore.

You can imagine the greatness of his wealth. Keep in mind, it all belonged to the King. As His Light-bearer, he was merely put in charge to manage it for Him. Because of the array of musical instruments built into him, every time he moved, the sweetest music flowed out of his being.

The King prepared a special "spot" for Light Bearer to begin his kingdom in Terra. It was the most beautiful and luxurious place. His mission was to make the entire Terra just like that original spot. The moment Light Bearer moved into this new territory, he began building his kingdom.

He built everything just like he saw it in the King's land. That was the King's order anyway. For some reason, he liked the north more than any other direction. So, he set up his throne on the farthest side of the north.

The kingdom began to grow in its power, glory and wealth, and everything became exactly as it was in the homeland.

Because Light Bearer could imagine and create anything he wanted within the limit he was permitted by the King, he began to produce innumerable products. And, as his business grew and spread across the land, so did his wealth and riches. As he established his kingdom and his throne was settled, he ruled it very well, and so the King was very pleased with him.

One day, as Light Bearer began to move around in his kingdom and saw all its glory and glitter, he said to himself, *Though I have everything I can imagine, and everything is just like in my King's country, I still lack one thing. In the King's country there are thousands and thousands of His servants singing and worshiping the King day and night. I know all about music and have been playing it for the glory and praise of the King. However, I don't think the King is honoring me sufficiently for what I have done for Him. Look at all this wealth and glory I have made for Him. I deserve to be praised and honored far more than what I am receiving right now.*

Thus he thought: *Look at what I have done. Look at all my wealth and riches. I have built a kingdom just like my King's. I have built great cities here at Terra; they are all mine. I have a throne, servants, and a territory. Why can't I be like the King? I know how He operates. I know enough of His mysteries that no one else knows about, so I deserve to be praised and worshiped just like the King!*.

However, from His far away land, the King perceived the thoughts in the Light Bearer's heart. He knew it was trouble, and that he was thinking such rebellious thoughts.

One thing about this King, is that He is very longsuffering and kind. He waits and gives plenty of chances to His servants and associates to repent and correct themselves in case they miss something. So,

CHAPTER 1 | HOW IT ALL BEGAN

He waited to give the Light Bearer the chance to renounce what was in his heart and not give in to it.

But the Light Bearer was not going to turn back. Rather, he influenced and appointed some of his associates to sing to him and praise him instead of the King. His associates thought it was fine because of his great accomplishments and display of power.

He began to call the cities and businesses after his own name. As time went by, he decided that he wanted more. He wanted to be just like the King. Not only to be like the King, but he wanted the very throne of the King, to rule the entire kingdom, just like the King ruled.

So, one day he called all of his servants and the mighty ones to help him. He explained to them what he was planning to do.

They all became very nervous and scared, because they knew no one could challenge the King, and no one could even think about defeating Him. There would be no contest; there was no point in even trying.

Nevertheless, the Light Bearer was convinced that he could dethrone the King, and no one could dissuade him sufficiently to get him to back off from his nefarious plan. The moment he entertained such diabolical thoughts in his heart, his wealth and wisdom became corrupted and it blinded him from seeing what was coming upon him if he tried to usurp the King as he planned.

They all had to listen to him because they were subject to him. If they did not listen to him he could harm them, so they agreed to follow him out of fear. Not only because of fear, but he promised them all great wealth and power, just like the King gave him Terra, once he took over the entire kingdom. Unfortunately, they all believed his lies.

The day came when they were all going to travel to their homeland, from where the King ruled His entire kingdom. They were all excited and ready to fight in case the King's army tried to stop them.

The King Himself, knew all of this already, and so as they moved closer, He ordered one of his mighty princes to fight the Light Bearer and defeat him and his servants. A great war broke out in the kingdom.

As I mentioned before, no one could defeat this King. Thus, the Light Bearer and his servants were cast out of the kingdom and were chased all the way back to Terra.

The King was angry because of what the Light Bearer tried to do. So, He destroyed everything that the Light Bearer had created. He sent a huge flood and wiped out everything he had achieved.

The cities and towns that were built by the Light Bearer were brought to the ground. Some of his servants were also destroyed, however, their spirits lingered around Terra, looking for any object that they could enter or possess. I say some, but the numbers were many.

The Light Bearer's kingdom was totally destroyed and Terra was completely covered with floodwaters. It became without form and void.

Since the Light Bearer was cut off, there was no source of light and Terra was filled with darkness. The King tied many of the servants of the Light Bearer in chains—those who were in charge of special projects and positions, and locked them up in a dark pit. Thus the anger of the King was subsided.

Light Bearer, who'd lost everything, was left alone with some of his servants who rebelled with him. But their form was totally altered because they lost the glory and favor of the King. There was nothing attractive about them as they stank every time they moved. Before, they were emanating different colors and lights whenever they moved, but now darkness became their abode. Nobody who saw them recognized who they were. They could not go back to the land of their King nor could they re-enter Terra because the King revoked all of their rights

CHAPTER 1 | HOW IT ALL BEGAN

and privileges. They had become as illegal wanderers, in their own lost kingdom, waiting for any opportunity to settle.

The Light Bearer was both very sad and angry with the King for what He had done. He was very bitter inside but didn't want to express it because he knew he would get into trouble again. So he waited in the space between Terra and the King's kingdom for a very long time, waiting for the King to do something about him or with the territory. But He knew that although everything he built had been destroyed, all of the wealth, precious stones, and metals still remained in Terra. No one took them. Given time, the waters would subside and then he could possess them again.

He was very clever. Although he'd lost all of his special abilities and wealth, the memories of what he'd done remained within him. He could re-create these, if he could take over some other beings whom the King would give the right to live and to have dominion over the span of Terra or any other new territory.

As time went by, the King called for another special meeting in His kingdom. This time He did not call all of His close associates. He only called His own family. He had many children, sons and daughters, and they all came to the meeting.

He told them, "I am concerned about Terra. Much of my wealth and resources are wasting away there. As a King, I do not like to waste anything I have. I need to utilize them. So I want you, My children, to go there and manage this place for Me. You know what happened to the Light Bearer. I do not want to give this place to any of my associates ever again. I want My own children to manage My kingdom for Me.

"I want My kingdom to continue to grow. I want My will to be done in Terra as it is in My kingdom. I want to regain and rebuild everything that was destroyed. Since you are My children with all the qualities I have, you will be able to re-create everything that was destroyed.

"I will restore Terra to its original creative order and make it ready for My children to live, grow, and expand. Because I am a King, everything that comes out of Me bears My imprint and quality. They will be kings over the entire region of Terra. I will give them power and authority over the Light Bearer and his forces, and they will be above them in rank and position.

"I want you to subdue and rule Terra, and exercise absolute dominion over it. The only thing I want from you, is to stay close to Me, listen, and do everything as I tell you, without Me you can do nothing."

All of His children were happy to hear their Father's plan. They sensed and were waiting for an opportunity to reign like their Father. They knew they were created for this, and one day it would happen. Now that time had come.

Somehow, the Light Bearer caught wind of all of these new movements in the far-away kingdom. When he found out that the King was planning to give his old territory of Terra to His own children, he wasn't happy. Fuming with jealousy and envy, he said within himself, *I will kill each one of them. I will take back everything I lost, because all the wealth and glory of Terra is mine.* He could not wait to have it all back under his control.

But he had to come up with a plan to kill the sons and daughters of the King. That would not be an easy task. He knew they were higher in rank and authority, and he was not ready for a face-to-face battle. For if he tried, it would be worse than the first attempt he'd made against the King. These sons and daughters of the King had another quality that the Light Bearer did not have; death and destruction had no power over them.

The Light Bearer schemed that the only way to get back what he had before was to somehow deceive these children of the King, and blind them to think all of the wealth and glory of Terra was not theirs, but his. He did not know how he was going to execute his treachery, so he waited patiently for the perfect time.

By His voice, the King decreed the restoration of Terra, and put it back into order. He moved all the water into one area, and He made the other part a habitable place for His children. Because they were His precious children, He did not want to be separated from them for too long. He loved them deeply and each one was so precious to Him. He did not send all of His children to Terra at once. He determined a specific time and place for each one when they should arrive in Terra, and how long they should live there.

So, the day came when the first son of the King was due to arrive in Terra. The King had prepared everything for His son to have a wonderful life. He prepared a special "spot" in Terra, just like in His kingdom, for His son to live; and his job was to duplicate it and cause it to grow.

Everything was peaceful and beautiful. The King had created other creatures to live with His children, and they were all in perfect harmony. He told him very specifically though, "You are My son and I am sending you there as a king. I want you to rule and to have dominion over it." His son's first responsibility was to be a king on this earth. He did not mention anything to His son about singing or making songs.

The Light Bearer hated this idea with all his guts. He never wanted any other king in Terra, let alone many kings. He couldn't imagine someone else ruling his old kingdom. That made him really furious.

However, another idea formed in his mind. If he could somehow take over these kings, then he could rule Terra once again through them! He could no longer wait for such a day to unleash his nefarious idea and execute his diabolic plan.

The children's assignment was to make Terra just like their Father's kingdom. Everything had to be done the way their Father showed them. Because Terra was an extension of their Father's kingdom, they had to keep any intruders out of Terra in case the Light Bearer or the ones that fell with him tried to enter and claim anything as theirs.

Because Terra was an extension of a kingdom, and hence the son of the King was also a king himself, he needed to act like a king. It was time for them to show their real nature to the creation around them. The King gave them rule over everything He created and their role was to make all of Terra look like their Father's kingdom.

The first son who arrived in Terra was not fully aware of the catastrophe that had once taken place there, as he was not aware of the footprints of those who once walked up and down on it. For some reason, he and the woman could not see or sense the danger lurking behind the trees.

They were mesmerized by the lushness and the sweetness around them. They knew in their heart that no one could defeat their Father, so they felt safe and didn't worry about any trouble coming. They did not understand the full implication of why their Father told them to have dominion and subdue the earth. That was chosen as the perfect opportunity which the Light Bearer was waiting for—to strike when they are not expecting any trouble. That's exactly what he did.

He deceived them with a cunning ploy, by using one of the creatures in Terra. He disguised himself in the creature and convinced them to disobey their Father. It was the worst nightmare the Father had ever encountered, and all of creation stood in shock and could not believe what had just happened in Terra—the biggest treason of all time had just taken place.

What broke the heart of the Father wasn't what His son did or what happened to him; he would have done anything to rescue and restore

CHAPTER 1 | HOW IT ALL BEGAN

him; but instead of running to Him for help and mercy, he identified with the Light Bearer, and thus became his slave because of fear.

The son whom the Father had appointed to work for Him now started working against Him. With further deceptions, the Light Bearer began to take over Terra and all of the wealth he once possessed. It had all belonged to the son, but the son wasn't able to comprehend its worth at all.

Once he fell into the trap of the Light Bearer, he lost his sense of his spirit and God-consciousness—his nature as a king and ruler; and so, everything changed. He began to walk around like a pauper who owned nothing. Once, he had been a son of the King, but subsequently turned himself into a beggar.

They lost the kingdom of their Father and began to work out something for living in the broken and dark kingdom of the Light Bearer. He started to use the sons of the King to establish his dark kingdom in Terra once again.

Despite this, the King was not going to let His children live in that condition forever. He had a plan to restore them to their original condition and position. The only way to do that was to defeat Light Bearer. Since it was one of His sons who gave the right to rule Terra to the Light bearer, it had to be one of His sons who should take it back from him.

The King had a very special Son through Whom all other sons and daughters were created. Not only the sons and daughters, but everything—visible or invisible—was created by this Son. The King knew this Son would do anything He bade him to do. He would go to any extent to accomplish anything His Father asked of Him.

The King called His beloved Son and presented to Him the plan of going to Terra to reconcile His brethren back to Him. The Son was happy because He always does the will of His Father.

The Son came to Terra and gave his life as a ransom for every lost son and daughter of the King, which are His brethren. He defeated the Light Bearer, and once again took all the rights and authority back from him. Now, the Light Bearer legally no longer had any rights or authority over any of the King's children, not even to oppress them.

The only condition the King made to His children, was whoever believed in His beloved Son, the King gave the right to become His children once again.

The King cannot love or do anything more than this for His children. Now it was up to His children to honor their King and His Son for what He had done by living a life of victory in Terra.

The King was successful restoring His children back as His sons and daughters, yet still today, His idea of restoring them as kings in Terra has been hindered by the Light Bearer and his minions. Any time a son comes up and tries to help others to enter into their dominion, one of the Light Bearer's servants will come with some kind of confusion or lies to try and keep them out of their purpose.

It is a sad dilemma, because of deception they keep on proclaiming, "This Terra is not ours, we are just passing through. All the wealth that was put in here belongs to someone else." The very purpose the King had put in all those resources in the earth for His sons and daughters has yet to be realized.

They are so busy with their many programs and fun activities, while the Light Bearer enjoys everything the King, their Father, had given to them to enjoy in Terra.

Many of His children are so poor, they can't even feed their own families. Many others die, never recognizing why they were put here by their Father. Many others of them are singing and making noises, because that's all they know to do.

CHAPTER 1 | HOW IT ALL BEGAN

The King waits for the day when His children will wake up from their sleep, and take back what rightly belongs to them; actually, what rightly belongs to their Father.

The King knows there is no need for anyone dying in Terra for lack of food or any other means. He has abundantly blessed Terra with everything they will ever need, no matter how many of His children live there at any given time.

So the most important task is restoring and releasing those children of the King as kings and queens of Terra back to His original intent; taking back and ruling what belongs to their Father's kingdom; to help those children of the King who are poor in Terra; to help the King reestablish His kingdom in Terra as it is in His homeland.

Unless these kings and queens are restored, those other children who have been deceived and oppressed by the Light Bearer will not be set free. The King will not do anything more regarding it, because He has done all that He needs to do, and has given the authority and power over Terra to His children, once and forever.

For the King and for His kingdom. Long live the King!

***

You may be wondering about some of the things you read in the story above and where I came up with it. Don't worry, almost everything I wrote is taken from the Bible. This book will prove it to you from Scripture.

In the story above, the King is our Father, Almighty God, Jehovah—the eternally existing One. His servants are angels and ministering spirits. The Light Bearer is Lucifer, who became Satan with his fall. The name *Lucifer* means "Light Bearer." He was also called the son of the morning (Isaiah 14:12). Terra is earth. The "spot" in both incidents is the garden of Eden. The word *Eden* means "a spot."

The King's sons and daughters are ourselves—human beings. His beloved Son is our Savior and Lord, Jesus Christ.

The purpose of the King to establish His kingdom on earth is yet to be realized. Jesus is waiting at the right hand of the Father until all His enemies are made His footstool. This teaching is intended to release those kings and queens to bring the enemies of God to Jesus' footstool.

One of His sons, and a king on earth, Abraham John

Chapter 2
THE REAL BEGINNING

Now, I would like to give you the biblical account of the allegory you have just read above.

The Bible begins, "In the beginning God created the heavens and the earth" (Genesis 1:1). This means that the heavens and the earth were created at the same time, which was in the beginning. If the earth had been created some one million years after the heavens were made, then they were not created in the beginning. We also understand from the Bible that mankind has been on this earth only a little more than six thousand years.

In the record of the six days of creation we read about in Genesis chapter one, we do not see God creating the earth or water because these were already in existence. If this is so, when and how did they get here?

Also, the Bible says God's works and His ways are perfect. He never creates anything that is empty, shapeless, or chaotic. However, in Genesis 1:2 we read, "The earth was without form, and void; and darkness was on the face of the deep. And the Spirit of God was hovering over the face of the waters."

What could have caused the earth to be in such a state? Why was the earth covered with water? I hope you remember what you read in the allegory earlier.

In Genesis we read that God looked at what He created and said, "It is good." However, the condition of the earth we see in verse two is anything but good!

If the heavens and the earth were created at the same time and the earth is as old as the heavens, was it ever inhabited by anyone other than human beings? If Lucifer fell from heaven to earth in eternity past, this earth had to be in existence then.

Scientists and archeologists have been discovering fossils and other items that are thousands and millions of years old, way before Adam was created. Where did these fossils come from? What were these creatures, and what happened to them? What kind of living situation did they have?

In Genesis 1:3-31, what God was doing was only rearranging and restoring the earth, making it once again habitable for the human beings He was planning to create.

Where do the fossils of dinosaurs and such animals come from? Were these all made up stories by archeologists? Some believe that dinosaurs lived before the flood of Noah.

If that's true, what they are saying is either God is a liar or Noah was a disobedient crook, because God told Noah to bring into the ark "every living thing of all flesh…male and female" (Genesis 6:19-20). We do not see God asking him to exclude dinosaurs. So, every creature that was alive *before* the flood, also existed *after* the flood.

On the very same day Noah and Noah's sons, Shem, Ham, and Japheth, and Noah's wife and the three wives of his

CHAPTER 2 | THE REAL BEGINNING

sons with them, entered the ark— they and every beast after its kind, all cattle after their kind, every creeping thing that creeps on the earth after its kind, and every bird after its kind, every bird of every sort. And they went into the ark to Noah, two by two, of all flesh in which *is* the breath of life. So those that entered, male and female of all flesh, went in as God had commanded him; and the Lord shut him in" – Genesis 7:13-16.

I hope you noticed the word *every* repeated four times to make sure that every creature that God created was brought onto the ark.

There is no evidence in the Bible that says the dinosaurs jumped out of the ark before the flood ended and committed suicide or were eaten by some other animals, or by Noah and his family. They did not have to eat the dinosaurs anyway, because God had told Noah to collect enough food for them and for the animals, and, most importantly, man only started eating animal meat *after* the flood (see Genesis 6:21-22; 9:3-4).

God created the earth for habitation. The Bible says in Isaiah 45:18, "For thus says the Lord, who created the heavens, who is God, who formed the earth and made it, who has established it, who did not create it in vain, who formed it to be inhabited: 'I am the Lord, and there is no other.'"

The verse above is talking about the original earth when God made it. There were inhabitants on this earth. I believe the earth was inhabited by other beings before the creation of human beings. If there were inhabitants on this earth, who were they, and what happened to them?

If human beings were the first inhabitants of this earth, how is it that demons come to live here before mankind?

Why did God allow Satan and demons to enter animals before the fall of man or before sin entered the earth?

Why did God tell Adam to *subdue* the fish of the sea, the fowls of the air, and every creeping thing that creeps on this earth?

How were they in any danger to Adam's existence on this earth? Why did he have to *subdue* them if there was no *rebellion*?

These are some of the questions I want you to think through with me and I will try to answer them in this chapter.

Only when we understand who Lucifer was, where he lived, and what his responsibilities were, will we understand his dealings with people on this earth today as our enemy. Ignorance of our enemy and how he operates can destroy us.

Lucifer's Origin

In two different accounts the Bible gives us a glimpse of how Lucifer was made, where he was, his qualities, abilities, responsibilities, and how he fell.

We are going to look at those Scriptures and learn a little bit about this magnificent creature which God created.

I believe the earth was inhabited by Lucifer and his associates. There is a multitude of evidence in the Bible to prove it, which I will share with you.

Their original purpose was to rule the earth, worship God, and expand His kingdom here. This is why I believe that after their fall, God created us to fill that place; we were created to rule the earth and to establish His kingdom.

There are some similar qualities and responsibilities which God gave to both Lucifer and to human beings.

Traditionally, the church has been teaching that Lucifer was created to worship God and that he was in heaven before he fell. The church also teaches that after Lucifer fell, God created human beings in that place to worship Him.

However, if Lucifer fell from heaven and we were created to replace him for worship, why were we not put in heaven?

If the devil can convince the church that their greatest responsibility on this earth is to worship (sing to) God, then he has somewhat succeeded in his mission, because as long as the church stays inside its four walls and sings about "I, me, and mine," or about flying away, it will never be a threat to his kingdom.

How and Why Lucifer was Created

We are going to see *how* and *why* God created Lucifer and what his responsibilities were. Please read on.

Whenever the Bible talks about Satan's identity, it talks about him being a king having a kingdom, never as a choir leader or a musician. It talks about him having access to heaven, but most of the times his operations are in relation to earth and its inhabitants. The Bible says that he has a kingdom (Matthew 12:26). If he has a kingdom, he is a king and he has a throne (Revelation 2:13).

Nevertheless, I am sure he was not ruling with God side by side in heaven. There is no way that could have ever happened. On the other hand, if he was not in charge of worship, then what was his responsibility? When did he become a king, where was he ruling as a king, and where did his kingdom exist?

We read in the Book of Revelation that Jesus said to the church in Pergamos the following lines,

> And to the angel of the church in Pergamos write, "These things says He who has the sharp two-edged sword: 'I know your works, and where you dwell, where Satan's throne *is*. And you hold fast to My name, and did not deny My faith even in the days in which Antipas *was* My faithful martyr, who was killed among you, where Satan dwells'" (Revelation 2:12-13).

In the verse above, Jesus said that Satan's throne was in *Pergamos* and that he dwelt there. This is quite interesting. As Pergamos was an ancient city located in the Anatolia region close to the Bergama, Izmir province of Turkey.

What was so special about this city that made Satan choose it to establish his throne and live there?

Pergamos was one of the most influential cities in those days. It was the center for politics, commerce, religion, the arts, and technology for all of Asia Minor. It was also a center for pagan worship, and was famous for the great altar of Zeus. That is the reason Satan chose this particular city to be the base of his operation. He knew that if he could influence Pergamos, he could control the entire region of Asia Minor.

This does not mean his throne is still in Pergamos and he lives there. In our time, however, he may have chosen one of the most influential cities of this world. It was normal at that time for nations to change the location of their capital based on who ruled it.

You may not believe or understand everything I say right away. The only thing I ask, is that you not stop reading yet. At the end everything will all make sense to you, as I will explain it more in detail.

Now, let's look at the passage of Scripture that talks about Lucifer from Ezekiel 28:12-16:

CHAPTER 2 | THE REAL BEGINNING

> Son of man, take up a lamentation for the king of Tyre, and say to him, 'Thus says the Lord God:"
>
> 'You were the seal of perfection, full of wisdom and perfect in beauty. You were in Eden, the garden of God; every precious stone was your covering: The sardius, topaz, and diamond, beryl, onyx, and jasper, sapphire, turquoise, and emerald with gold.
>
> The workmanship of your timbrels and pipes was prepared for you on the day you were created.
>
> You were the anointed cherub who covers; I established you; you were on the holy mountain of God; you walked back and forth in the midst of fiery stones.
>
> You were perfect in your ways from the day you were created, till iniquity was found in you.
>
> By the abundance of your trading you became filled with violence within, and you sinned; therefore I cast you as a profane thing out of the mountain of God; and I destroyed you, O covering cherub, from the midst of the fiery stones."

The verses above had an immediate application to the king of Tyre, whose name is not mentioned. Like most Scriptures in the Bible, these also have a spiritual application.

From the verses above we learn the following: Most of the descriptions of the person (or being) mentioned above clearly show that it is not talking about an ordinary (human) being.

No king ever lived in the garden of Eden except for Adam. No human king ruled from the mountain of God. No one was a seal of perfection, full of wisdom, and perfect in beauty. It also says in verse fourteen that this person or being was an anointed cherub.

The noun *cherub* appears thirty times in the New King James Version of the Bible. Cherubs are one type of spiritual-being mentioned in the Bible, and they are not humans. Twenty-nine times it is talking about spirit-beings, and one time as the name of a place in Babylon.

Bible scholars believe that this passage describes Lucifer and what happened to him. The verses above say that he was the seal of perfection, meaning everything about him and everything he did was perfect. He was full of wisdom and perfect in beauty, covered with every precious stone. He was residing in Eden, the garden of God (which was on this earth). He was anointed by God. His place was on the holy mountain of God.

The book of Ezekiel shows where the garden of Eden is at present:

> I made the nations shake at the sound of its fall, when I cast it down to hell together with those who descend into the Pit; and all the trees of Eden, the choice and best of Lebanon, all that drink water, were comforted in the depths of the earth – Ezekiel 31:16.

> To which of the trees in Eden will you then be likened in glory and greatness? Yet you shall be brought down with the trees of Eden to the depths of the earth –Ezekiel 31:18.

The two verses above tell us that the trees of Eden (garden) are now under the earth. I believe it happened during the second flood that we read about in Genesis chapters six to eight. Until that time, it was kept and protected by cherubim with flaming swords (Genesis 3:24).

Though the person here is symbolized as the king of Tyre, from the description we know that no human king on this earth was created by God like this one. God does not call a human king *an anointed cherub*. According to verse thirteen of the same chapter, Lucifer was in the garden of Eden, while the Bible clearly says the garden of Eden was on this earth.

In God's kingdom there are various types of spirit-beings with different responsibilities. There are angels of various ranks, ministering spirits, then seraphim, cherubim, living creatures, and human beings.

Of these, cherubim are the closest in proximity to God, as their job is to cover and to expand God's glory. Hence, they know more about God and His glory than any other creature He has made.

The second thing the Bible says in verse fourteen, is that Lucifer was on the holy mountain of God, walking back and forth in the midst of fiery stones.

Where is the holy mountain of God? The first place the phrase *holy mountain of God* appears in the Bible is in Exodus 3:1 where Moses led the sheep up to the mountain of God.

Wherever the phrase *holy mountain* or *mountain of God* is mentioned in the Bible, it always refers to a mountain that is on the earth, it is not talking about any mountain in heaven.

This third description given is of Lucifer walking back and forth in the midst of the fiery stones on the mountain. We also see this in the book of Exodus. When God came down on the mountain to meet with Moses, the Bible says under his feet were like sapphire stones shining with fire on top of the mountain. Ezekiel 28:13 talks about Lucifer having sapphire stones as his covering.

> Then Moses went up, also Aaron, Nadab, and Abihu, and seventy of the elders of Israel, and they saw the God of Israel. And there was under His feet as it were a paved work of sapphire stone, and it was like the very heavens in its clarity —Exodus 24:9-10.

> The sight of the glory of the Lord was like a consuming fire on the top of the mountain in the eyes of the children of Israel —Exodus 24:17.

God did not bring down a mountain from heaven. These verses are talking about a mountain on this earth where God came down to meet with Moses. I will explain more about the location of Lucifer in the following lines of this chapter.

Ezekiel 28:13 says, "The workmanship of your timbrels and pipes was prepared for you on the day you were created." The first human being whom God created was Adam, and He had not created any special kings before that. This is the verse that people use to describe that Lucifer was in charge of worship in heaven. He was covered with precious stones and musical instruments were built into his body. He was a flying orchestra.

However, that is not all we read about what Lucifer did in these verses.

Now we are going to look at the qualities, abilities, and responsibilities Lucifer had when God created him, and the sins he committed before his fall.

The Qualities of Lucifer

1. He was perfect (Ezekiel 28:12). First of all, he was the seal of perfection, full of wisdom and beauty.

Let us do a word study on these to see what they actually mean in the Hebrew language. The word used for perfect is *kaliyl* meaning "entire, all, perfect."[1]

---

[1] The Online Bible Thayer's Greek Lexicon and Brown Driver & Briggs Hebrew Lexicon.

CHAPTER 2 | THE REAL BEGINNING

2. He was full of wisdom and beauty (Ezekiel 28:12). The word used for wisdom is *chokmah* meaning "skill (in war), wisdom (in administration), shrewdness, wisdom, prudence (in religious affairs), wisdom (ethical and religious)."[2]

If Lucifer's only responsibility was to worship God, then why did he need skill in war, wisdom to administer, and other qualities mentioned above?

The word *chokmah* can refer to technical skills or special abilities in fashioning something. The first occurrence of *chokmah* is in Exodus 28:3 (KJV), "And thou shalt speak unto all that are wise hearted, whom I have filled with the spirit of wisdom, that they may make Aaron's garments to consecrate him, that he may minister unto me in the priest's office."[3]

3. He was covered with nine precious stones (Ezekiel 12:13). Lucifer was covered with nine precious stones. He was in charge of the wealth of God's kingdom.

The number nine is a significant number in Scripture. It is the last of the single digits, so it represents finality or the conclusion of a matter. It also signifies judgment.

There are nine fruit of the Spirit and nine fruit of wisdom. The fruit of *chokmah*, wisdom, are many, and the book of Proverbs describes the characters of the *chakam* and *chokmah* wisdom. In New Testament terms, the *fruit of wisdom* are the same as the fruit of the Holy Spirit. "But the fruit of the Spirit is love, joy, peace, longsuffering, kindness,

---

[2] The Online Bible Thayer's Greek Lexicon and Brown Driver & Briggs Hebrew Lexicon.

[3] Vine's Expository Dictionary of Biblical Words, Copyright © 1985, Thomas Nelson Publishers.

goodness, faithfulness, gentleness, self-control: against such there is no law" – Galatians 5:22-23.[4]

Look at what James says about the traits of wisdom:

> But the wisdom that is from above is first pure, then peaceable, gentle, and easy to be entreated, full of mercy and good fruits, without partiality, and without hypocrisy. And the fruit of righteousness is sown in peace of them that make peace – James 3:17-18 KJV.

4. Musical instruments were built in him (Ezekiel 28:13). The Bible says that he had "tabrets" built into him. When he flew, the air in the atmosphere would produce the greatest music ever played in this universe. The four corners of the earth echoed that music and all spirit beings on this earth resonated in harmony and worshiped God and gave Him praise.

Isaiah 14:7 (KJV) says:

> The whole earth is at rest and quiet; they break forth into singing.

This is why there are more ungodly musicians on this earth than godly ones.

5. He was in charge of innovation, manufacturing, and the development of God's kingdom (Ezekiel 28:13). The word *workmanship* in Hebrew is *melakah*, which means "occupation, work, business." Thayer's Lexicon gives these meanings to the word: "property; work (something done or made); workmanship; service or use; public business, political or religious."[5]

---

[4] Vine's Expository Dictionary of Biblical Words, Copyright © 1985, Thomas Nelson Publishers.

[5] The Online Bible Thayer's Greek Lexicon and Brown Driver & Briggs Hebrew Lexicon.

CHAPTER 2 | THE REAL BEGINNING

The Hebrew word for *pipes* is even more interesting. It is *neqeb*, which means "groove, socket, hole, cavity, settings," and is a technical term relating to a jeweler's work.[6] This is the only place this particular word is used in the entire Bible. I thought this word represented a musical instrument, but it does not.

6. He was full of light or brightness (Ezekiel 28:17). The earth depended on the brightness of Lucifer for its light. The word used for *Lucifer* in the Hebrew language is *heylel*, which means "light-bearer" and it has the following meanings:

> 1) The shining one, the morning star, Lucifer; used of the king of Babylon and Satan (figuratively);

> 2) Theological Wordbook of the Old Testament: `Helel,' describing the king of Babylon.[7]

> 3) The Hebrew word used for brightness is *yiph`ah*, which means "splendor, brightness, or shining."[8]

In the New Testament, Paul says that Satan transforms himself into an angel of light (2 Corinthians 11:14). He was full of light and brightness, and that is why I said that planet earth did not need any terrestrial light before the creation of man.

When he fell his light became darkness. That is why the earth became full of darkness and he became the ruler of darkness. His kingdom is now called the kingdom of darkness.

---

6 The Online Bible Thayer's Greek Lexicon and Brown Driver & Briggs Hebrew Lexicon.

7 The Online Bible Thayer's Greek Lexicon and Brown Driver & Briggs Hebrew Lexicon.

8 The Online Bible Thayer's Greek Lexicon and Brown Driver & Briggs Hebrew Lexicon.

God created the sun, moon, and stars later to light up the earth and sky. In the new earth and new heaven there will not be any sun and moon. The glory of Jesus will be its light day and night (Revelation 22:5).

Lucifer's Abilities

These include the following:

To expand the trade and business of God on this planet:

> By the multitude of thy merchandise they have filled the midst of thee with violence, and thou hast sinned: therefore I will cast thee as profane out of the mountain of God: and I will destroy thee, O covering cherub, from the midst of the stones of fire – Ezekiel 28:16 KJV.

The Hebrew word used for *merchandise* in this verse is *rekulla*, which means "merchandize, traffic, or trade."[9]

He was in charge of business and the growth of God's kingdom and wealth on this earth. He manufactured products and filled the earth with these products and trade. His job was to transform God's ideas into manifestation or to materialize the thoughts of God in this natural world.

He was excellent as a musician and in business (Ezekiel 28:13,18)[10]

He had the ability to produce things (Ezekiel 28:16). The wisdom he had was *chokmah* wisdom, which also means the ability to imagine and make things.

---

9 The Online Bible Thayer's Greek Lexicon and Brown Driver & Briggs Hebrew Lexicon.

10 Refer to points 4 and 5 of the Qualities of Lucifer for more information.

He could walk and travel freely in this universe (Ezekiel 28:14). In Job 1:6-7, we read that Satan was roaming around the earth. He had access to heaven and the presence of God.

Lucifer's Responsibilities

From the verses above we understand that Lucifer was responsible for the business, wealth, development, and worship in God's kingdom on this earth.

He was an anointed cherub. The word for *anointed* in Hebrew is *mimshach,* and this is the only place it is used in the entire Bible. It means "expansion or spread."[11]

It is interesting to notice that Lucifer was anointed to cover, spread, and expand swiftly. In other words, the devil was a cherub of expansion. The purposes of God that related to this earth—His glory, wisdom, abilities, and wealth—were all in Lucifer's hands to expand these on this earth.

This is why whatever the devil and his children do on this earth grows and spreads quickly, while we are struggling to grow our ministries and businesses. It's not because we lack ideas, but because we lack the anointing for growth and expansion.

If you watch the media today you will hardly hear any positive news. All we hear about is the evil that is going on in the world. Music, movies, or any product that supports the devil and his kingdom quickly spreads worldwide; while we store our plans, books, products, and music in a garage or in boxes somewhere.

---

11 The Online Bible Thayer's Greek Lexicon and Brown Driver & Briggs Hebrew Lexicon.

We do not know what it takes to expand and spread, while worldly people can write any nonsense and it will spread and become a best seller. It is the combination of *chokma* wisdom and the *mimshach* anointing of their god (the devil is the god of this world) that works for them.

Lucifer corrupted his anointing and wisdom, and now it no longer accomplishes God's purpose, but his own. We are not going to wait any longer. Since we have now come to know their secret, we can receive that same *mimshach* anointing from God, and spread out worldwide in Jesus' name.

That is why Jesus told us to be wise as serpents and harmless as doves (Matthew 10:16). He wants us to master the wisdom God gave to the serpent and use it for God's kingdom purpose.

Lucifer was in charge of the development and growth of God's kingdom. When God decided to do something new, it was Lucifer who executed it. He was in charge of all business, trade, innovation, manufacturing, and marketing in a world that we know very little about, but there are many more clues in the verses that we are going to examine below.

He was the anointed Cherub that covers. Cherubim are the closest to God. One of their jobs is to protect or cover God's glory. It is almost like a personal bodyguard, though God would not need such a one. Even today, Lucifer does the same job, but now instead of protecting God's glory, he covers or blinds us from seeing God's kingdom and His glory.

This is why the New Testament says, "The god of this world blinds (covers) the minds of the unbelievers" (2 Corinthians 4:4). Sometimes, he even blinds believers from seeing what God has prepared or done for them (Ephesians 4:17-18). If you are blinded to any truth, know that it is not the Spirit of God Who hinders you, but the spirit of this world.

He had abundance of business and trade (Ezekiel 28:18). Again, the scripture says Lucifer did trading on this earth and increased in wealth and splendor. *Trade* means he did business on this earth. There were nations and kingdoms on this earth that were built by him and his associates according to Isaiah 14:16-17.

There were spiritual beings that were inferior to Lucifer in rank on this earth and with him, animals like dinosaurs and suchlike. Just like the earth today, human beings are the spiritual beings and we have scores of animals and other creatures on this earth, which we call the animal kingdom.

Lucifer's Sins

We have heard that Lucifer fell because of his pride, but there's more to this story. There were four reasons (sins) that he became prideful and fell.

1) Iniquity. Ezekiel 28:15 says:

> You were perfect in your ways from the day you were created, till *iniquity* was found in you.

Because of his perfection, wisdom, and wealth he became haughty and crooked. The Hebrew word used for *iniquity* is *evel* or `*avel* which means "Injustice, unrighteousness, wrong; a)   violent deeds of injustice; b) injustice (used of speech); c) injustice (generally)."[12]

---

12 The Online Bible Thayer's Greek Lexicon and Brown Driver & Briggs Hebrew Lexicon.

I believe he began to boast about his abilities and perfection, which led to self-exaltation. This is why the Bible says not to think too highly of yourself (Romans 12:3).

2) Violence. The second sin of Lucifer was violence. I do not think he would have expressed any of these if he was in heaven. Ezekiel 28:16 says:

> By the abundance of your trading you became filled with *violence* within, and you sinned.

The Hebrew word used for *violence* is *chamac,* which means "violence, wrong, cruelty, injustice."[13] He increased his wealth greatly through his trade, and became blind to his own destruction and greed. He may have started to treat his subordinates with cruelty, like a dictator.

In the Old Testament, when God instituted kings to rule Israel, one restriction given was not to multiply gold, silver, and other types of wealth (Deuteronomy 17:17). In Genesis (6:13) we read that before the flood of Noah, the earth was filled with violence because of the wickedness of men, which led God to destroy the earth once again.

3) Pride and Corruption. Ezekiel 28:17 says:

> Your heart was lifted up because of your beauty; you corrupted your wisdom for the sake of your splendor.

We all know this part. He became prideful because of his beauty. He was a magnificent creature with extraordinary abilities and beauty which led him to be prideful. He corrupted the wisdom God gave him to execute His will on this earth, and began to use it to propagate evil in the world.

---

13 The Online Bible Thayer's Greek Lexicon and Brown Driver & Briggs Hebrew Lexicon.

CHAPTER 2 | THE REAL BEGINNING

He corrupted his wisdom for sake of his own prosperity or splendor. There are nations and leaders currently on the earth who characteristically operate in a similar fashion as mentioned here. You can imagine the spirit that works behind them.

There were kings in Israel who became prideful, and departed from His ways when God blessed them.

4) Defilement. Ezekiel 28:18 says:

> You defiled your sanctuaries by the multitude of
> your iniquities.

The Hebrew word used for *defile* is *chalal,* which means "1) To profane, to defile, to pollute, to desecrate, to begin to profane oneself ritually, sexually; 2) To be polluted, to be defiled."[14]

We read in 1 Samuel how the sons of Eli despised and defiled the sanctuary of God by stealing the sacrifices and sleeping with women at the door of the tabernacle (1 Samuel 2:17, 22).

Now we have an idea about what kind of being Lucifer was. He was cunning and shrewd in business, and had great beauty and wisdom. He could imagine and create almost anything he wanted.

Keep in mind that this particular cherub which God created had a free will like you and I. He was in charge of all of heaven's business (wealth) and energy related to our universe! Though he sinned, he is still anointed, with the only exception being that his anointing and wisdom are now corrupted. As I mentioned earlier, he wanted to be like God and rule the earth and heaven. He was looking for an opportunity.

---

14 The Online Bible Thayer's Greek Lexicon and Brown Driver & Briggs Hebrew Lexicon.

You might be wondering why I write about Lucifer in a book about kings and queens. If you do not know where you came from and why you were put on this earth, you will never be able to discover and fulfill your purpose and full potential.

Statistics say that more than ninety-percent (90%) of the people on earth do not know why they are here. So, you can imagine the confusion people in this world are going through.

Now, we are going to learn about how Lucifer became Satan, or the devil, as we know him today.

Chapter 3
THE FALL OF LUCIFER

Imagine in the ageless past, one day Lucifer flying in mid-air above Earth, enjoying his new planet and the glory that was given to him. He heard countless numbers of angelic beings singing and worshiping the great King day and night. He saw the abundance of blessing and the glory of this great kingdom. He saw the great cities and golden palaces he and other creatures had built on the earth.

The atmosphere of the earth was as the Bible says in Isaiah 14:7, "The whole earth is at rest, and is quiet; they break forth into singing."

Lucifer's Four Levels of leadership

Lucifer had four levels of leadership working under him. The first were *principalities*, which were in charge of nations and territories, and were directly responsible to him. Then, he had *powers*. These were heads of different components (like economy, justice, health) of international or global organizations that oversaw nations, like we have the UN, IMF, ICJ and other organizations.

Then came *rulers* which became rulers of different nations. These were local leaders and authorities working under powers. And fourthly, he had *armies of spirit beings* who took care of the day-to-day affairs of the local territories. After the fall, they are called spiritual wicked forces in heavenly places (see Ephesians 6:12).

For whatever reason, he was not as happy as he used to be. He had a different feeling he never had before. His heart was not in what he was doing as it used to be.

He began to wonder. *What is in this for me? I have developed and built all these kingdoms and nations. I do not feel I get the amount of respect and credit that is due someone like me. I can do these things my own way and all this planet is given unto me. I am greater than all these angels and they all respect and obey me. I do not want to be accountable to anyone. What if I declare my dominion over this planet and make it my kingdom? I will receive the worship and adoration that is given to the great King and all the wealth and resources in it will become mine to enjoy.*

Days and years went by, and when he prepared music to be sung by the angels, he slowly began to put his name into one or two places. He did not put his name in directly, instead he made up names for himself and inserted them. He is not only known as Lucifer or Satan on this earth today, but is also known by scores of names of false gods and goddesses.

At first, he did not foresee any danger in doing it because he was in charge of the planet and did not feel he did anything wrong. Plus, the angels and spirit beings didn't know it either. For a while, he felt good when he heard the angels singing his name. It brought a special feeling he'd never felt before, and it made him feel better than the other angels. The more he heard his name praised, the more he wanted to hear it again. Because he didn't sense any immediate reaction from the King, he thought everything was working out for his benefit.

When his business grew and merchandise and trade was multiplied, so did his wealth. He began to hoard it for himself, and began

CHAPTER 3 | THE FALL OF LUCIFER

to demand more and more from his associates, becoming a tyrant that ruled by force and demanded respect.

How do I know this? It says so in the Bible, which I explained under the heading *Sins of Lucifer*. He began to use violence to accomplish his evil purposes.

As days went by, he became greedier to get praise, and so he started to insert his name in almost everything that was done on the earth. He began to exalt himself into a new position. The angels that were with him were a little scared about this change, but they had no power to question him. They were to submit to him because he was their ruler.

Slowly, he began to feel that he was better than the great King Himself, and that he also deserved to be praised and adored, just like the King. He began to direct the singing and adoration that was only given to the King, towards himself. He desired to have all the wealth and glory of this earth for himself.

The King knew about the change that was taking place in Lucifer. Notwithstanding, because He is longsuffering and foreknew what was coming, He waited to see what choices Lucifer would make regarding this new turn of events. It is not honorable for a benevolent King to interfere with someone's choice or will.

Now, we are going to look at the passage from Isaiah chapter fourteen to see the fall of Lucifer:

> How you are fallen from heaven, O Lucifer, son of the morning! How you are cut down to the ground, you who weakened the nations!
>
> For you have said in your heart: 'I will ascend into heaven, I will exalt my throne above the stars of God; I will also sit on the mount of the congregation on the farthest sides of

the north; I will ascend above the heights of the clouds, I will be like the Most High.'

Yet you shall be brought down to Sheol, to the lowest depths of the Pit. Those who see you will gaze at you, and consider you, saying: 'Is this the man who made the earth tremble, who shook kingdoms, Who made the world as a wilderness and destroyed its cities, who did not open the house of his prisoners?' – Isaiah 14:12-17.

Verse twelve starts like this: "How are you fallen from heaven, O Lucifer, son of the morning!" He was cut down to the ground and he also weakened the nations. How did he get to heaven?

Which nations did he weaken, and what ground is this verse talking about?

The answer to that question is mentioned in verses thirteen and fourteen, where it says, "For you have said in your heart: 'I will ascend into heaven…I will ascend above the heights of the clouds.'"

If he was ascending to heaven, then he was not in heaven. When he fell, he was ascending into heaven. When he fell, to where did he fall?

Verse twelve has that answer. It says, "How are you cut down to the ground."

The Hebrew word used for *heaven* is *shamayim* (shaw-mah'-yim), which means to be lofty, the sky (as aloft; the dual perhaps alluding to the visible arch in which the clouds move, as well as to the higher ether where the celestial bodies revolve)."[15]

---

[15] Biblesoft's New Exhaustive Strong's Numbers and Concordance with Expanded Greek-Hebrew Dictionary.

CHAPTER 3 | THE FALL OF LUCIFER

The Hebrew word used for "to ascend" is *alah* (aw-law'); meaning "to ascend, intransitively (be high), or actively (mount); used in a great variety of senses, primary and secondary, literal and figurative (as follow): arise (up), (cause to) ascend up, at once, break [the day] (up), bring (up), (cause to) burn, carry up, cast up, shew, climb (up), (cause to, make to) come (up), cut off, dawn, depart, exalt, excel, fall, fetch up, get up, (make to) go (away, up); grow (over) increase, lay, leap, levy, lift (self) up, light, [make] up, mention, mount up, offer, make to pay, perfect, prefer, put (on), raise, recover, restore, (make to) rise (up), scale, set (up), shoot forth (up), (begin to) spring (up), stir up, take away (up), work."[16]

The Hebrew word used for *ground* is same as the word used for *earth* in verse sixteen and elsewhere in the Bible.

From the Scriptures above, it is clear that Lucifer was not in heaven. He was cut down when he was ascending into heaven, and when he fell, he was cut down to the ground, which is earth.

Verse sixteen says, "Is this the man who made the earth tremble, who shook kingdoms, who made the world as a wilderness and destroyed its cities?" This verse clearly describes the condition of the earth before Genesis 1:2, and how it became the way it did in verse two of Genesis chapter one.

Some say Lucifer was sent to the garden of Eden as an angel to minister to Adam and Eve, who later then transgressed against God when he tempted them. You cannot prove this from the Bible itself.

If he transgressed while he was in the garden with Adam and Eve, then when was he on the mountain of God as a king on this earth and doing trade? Where do all other evil spirits come from?

---

16 Biblesoft's New Exhaustive Strong's Numbers and Concordance with Expanded Greek-Hebrew Dictionary.

One day Lucifer called his key leaders and expressed his true feelings to them. They were sympathetic toward what he felt. He told them they had been working for years, and it was not fair that only the King got all the praise and worship.

After all, *they* are the ones who built all of those magnificent palaces and cities. So, they also deserved to be praised. He was ruling the great planet, and he said he was also a king. He laid out a plan before them to run a coup to dethrone the King and take over the whole universe. Then they would coerce all the rest of the angels to side with them. He promised them special positions when he came into power, and they could rule from the King's palace itself.

Lucifer could go into the presence of God, as we see in the book of Job. He used his access to heaven to influence other angels of God. One third of them joined in his revolt against God. Those angels who joined with Lucifer lost their heavenly positions. However, they are not roaming this earth attacking humans, as many believe and teach. In the Bible, we read about fallen angels that they are *kept* in the abyss for the day of judgment.

Evidently, the day came, and the plot for the revolt was in place. As if they were going to worship the King, they began to ascend into the heavens. The King knew their plan and exactly what was going to happen. As Lucifer and his cohorts were ascending into heaven, He called His warrior princes and informed them of the plot. He commanded them to cast Lucifer and his associates down from their positions. Lucifer was not willing to surrender, for he had made up his mind to do his own will, even if this meant that he had to fight with the King and His princes.

A great battle broke out in heaven, and the King and His princes won. As a result, Lucifer and his friends were cast down, and they fell to earth like lightning.

They could never return to their original positions on this earth. In revenge, and with great wrath, he and his associates destroyed all the kingdoms and nations that were on this earth.

Jesus, Himself, said, "I saw Satan fall like lightning from heaven" – Luke 10:18.

Isaiah 14:12b states:

> How you are cut down to the ground, you who weakened the nations!

And, Isaiah 14:16b-17 continues with:

> Is this the man who made the earth tremble, who shook kingdoms, who made the world as a wilderness and destroyed its cities, who did not open the house of his prisoners?

The King commanded that all the angels which rebelled with Lucifer should be bound and kept in darkness until the Day of Judgment (2 Peter 2:4; Jude 1:6). These were mighty angels, strong in power and wisdom. They could do great damage if they were released on this earth.

There were other creatures on the earth which existed during Lucifer's reign. These no longer respected the King, nor honored His kingdom on the earth. They began a new order of worship and gave honor to Lucifer. They began to change the system on the earth. Great cities and nations were destroyed and darkness filled the earth.

The King saw that the earth was no longer fit for the place where His will was done as in heaven. He grieved over the creatures He had made on the earth, and decided to destroy everything with a great flood.

God destroyed that world with a flood, and all the creatures which were created to serve Lucifer and his kingdom also perished; as their natures had also become corrupted by associating with Lucifer.

Their bodies perished in the flood, but their spirits did not. Their spirits were disconnected from the King, and became evil in nature, and thus they later became evil or unclean spirits (demons) on this earth. Their spirits began to roam the atmosphere of this earth looking for habitation. That is how the earth became formless and void, filled with darkness.

The earth was greatly impacted by this revolt, which marred its beauty and the perfection it once had. Lucifer could not reestablish his kingdom on the earth. Though he had access, he had lost his authority and rights over the earth. So, he stayed mid-air between the earth and heaven.

Thus it says in Genesis 1:2, "The earth was without form, and void; and the darkness was on the face of the deep. And the Spirit of God was hovering over the face of the waters."

The King did not totally give up on the earth though. He knew His will would be done on the earth again as it was in the beginning. Other angels in heaven looked at Lucifer and began to regret what happened to him saying, "How you are fallen from heaven, O Lucifer, son of the morning! How art thou cut down to the ground, you who weakened the nations!" (Isaiah 14:12).

This affected Lucifer more than anything. His nature was completely corrupted and he lost his glory and splendor. He became full of darkness instead. Sin and rebellion had entered his being, and he became an enemy of the great King.

Everyone associated with him inherited the same nature. He was kicked out of God's kingdom because his nature was corrupted with sin. He and his cohorts waited for another opportune time to take over the earth and pay the King back for what He had done to him.

He was not regretful of what he had done, nor was he willing to repent, for his pride made him feel that it was the right thing. His name was no longer Lucifer; it became *Satan*, which means "adversary."

If Lucifer was in heaven, he could not have sinned, because there is perfection in heaven, and there is no sin. He was in a different realm than heaven where God dwells; he was on the earth in its original form and beauty.

God judged the earth and He destroyed that world with a flood. It resulted in the destruction of the earth and all that was in it. The archeological findings of fossils and other remnants that are millions of years old are from that prehistoric civilization only.

Satan could no longer establish his kingdom on this earth. The earth is a physical world and only those with physical bodies can remain on it and do anything legally. So he established his kingdom above the earth. That is why the Bible calls him the prince of the power of the air (Ephesians 2:2). He could not come back to earth because it was flooded, and he could not go to heaven.

When God destroyed the then-inhabited world, all the animals and spiritual beings (they had physical bodies) were destroyed, but their spirits remained on this earth waiting for physical bodies to re-enter. This is why God told Adam to *subdue* the earth and its creatures. For whatever reason, God allowed those evil spirits to enter creatures of this earth before the fall of mankind. They are the evil spirits, or demons, on this earth today.

The Eden of Lucifer was destroyed by the first flood, and thus the earth became empty, void, and full of darkness.

The reason why the devil and those spirits could not come back to earth was because they each needed a physical body (either human or animal) to operate through in the physical realm. The earth was covered with water and there was no physical object that could be seen. Sometimes these spirits can enter into other physical substances besides living organisms.

So, they stayed in the second heaven (the invisible realm, spiritual realm, or heavenly places) and made that their abode. They waited until God restored the earth before reentering physical substances or other living organisms.

This is why the devil had access to this earth and the garden of Eden before the fall of man. Though God judged them, He did not sentence them to their eternal punishment yet. As we see in the Gospels, demons requested that Jesus not to judge them before the time (Matthew 8:29).

I do not believe demons are fallen angels, because the Bible says those angels that were fallen, or had sinned; are bound and kept awaiting their judgment. For example:

For if God did not spare the angels who sinned, but cast them down to hell and delivered them into chains of darkness, to be reserved for judgment. – 2 Peter 2:4

> And the angels who did not keep their proper domain, but left their own abode, He has reserved in everlasting chains under darkness for the judgment of the great day. – Jude 6

In addition, four of those angels will be released for a short while to kill mankind, at the end of time:

> Saying to the sixth angel who had the trumpet, 'Release the four angels who are bound at the great river Euphrates.' So the four angels, who had been prepared for the hour

CHAPTER 3 | THE FALL OF LUCIFER

and day and month and year, were released to kill a third of mankind. – Revelation 9:14-15

The Bible never addresses demons or evil spirits as fallen angels. If the demons we cast out from people were angels, we would not be able to cast them out. We do not yet have power over angels, neither do we have authority to judge them right now, but we will in future (1 Corinthians 6:3).

Angels are much more powerful than human beings. One angel of God killed 185,000 humans in one night (2 Kings 19:35). Jesus never mentioned angels when He was dealing with demonic spirits. He always addressed them as demons or evil spirits.

There are different kinds of spirit-beings, and angels are one of them. Jesus addressed demons as evil spirits. Demonic spirits are beings lesser in authority and power than angels and human spirits.

Demonic spirits are the disembodied spirits of those fallen spirit-beings from the pre-Adamic world. God allowed those spirits to remain on this earth for whatever reason (I believe it is because the earth was their original abode) before the creation of Adam.

I believe it is so because God gave this earth (stewardship) first to them to rule and to have dominion over. God decided to restore the earth and create another spiritual being, called a human being, to rule and to have dominion.

This man then, had to subdue not only the planet, but also the spiritual rebellion that was already going on—the one on this earth. This is God's absolute will for every single human being: to have dominion and authority over the earth. Both will be on this earth until this present world is destroyed totally by fire.

What Lucifer wanted was the worship and the wealth that belongs to God; and now, through unsaved and blinded human beings he receives these for a while. The devil and his kingdom (through unregenerate human beings) manage the majority of the wealth today.

In the Bible we see people worshiping a fish as their god. In Greek mythology, birds were objects of worship. In some Asian countries, people worship cattle and other animals as gods.

It is interesting to see that the four categories of creatures God told Adam to subdue and take dominion over, are objects of worship in some part of the world. Although, they are not actually worshiping these creatures themselves, but rather the spirits they represent. I have also personally seen that when demons manifest in people they act like different creatures and animals. There is a reason for this manifestation.

Animals do not go to heaven, as some might think. When I came to the West I saw people treating their pets like they treat a person, or even better. I have seen demon-possessed animals including cats, dogs, cows, etc. Sometimes these spirits manifest through animals, and so they bite and attack human beings; and if they do not receive treatment they will eventually die.

Most animals do not have the concept of family or a moral conscious like humans do. They do not have shame or guilt like human beings. I have noticed that in any culture where animals were treated like people or gods and people do everything with them as they would with humans; and then those people also behave like animals. Idol worship, incest, and bestiality are the result of animal love.

It is the intention of the enemy to bring human beings down to the level of animals. In some countries, animals have more rights and privileges than human beings! I have seen people who have soul ties with their pets, and cannot go anywhere without them. I am not against having pets, but if the pets *have* you instead of you having the pet, then it is a problem.

Bestiality is a growing problem in different cultures of the world. Incest has destroyed millions of lives and continues to destroy many families; and that happens when man loses his human consciousness, and adopts an animal consciousness—doing what is right in their own minds. When you spend time with something or someone, eventually you will become like that thing or person.

The Bible says if you walk with the wise you will become wise (Proverbs 13:20) and if you walk with the foolish you will act foolish.

It is sad to hear that people spend more money on their pets than they spend for preaching the gospel and caring for the poor around the world. It is time to take dominion over the things and creatures that God said in the beginning to subdue. Otherwise, they will take dominion over you.

It is interesting to note that whenever evil people dress up for carnivals or parades, they always dress up like an animal or a bird. Please do not get offended, this is the truth; and truth is hard—sometimes it hurts.

Another reason why people worship animals as gods is because of the close relationship the demonic world has with them. The Bible describes Satan as a *beast* and a *serpent* in the book of Revelation. The Bible also compares birds, animals, and creeping things to evil spirits.

When the devil came to tempt Eve, he entered a serpent and disguised himself as a creature that was familiar to her. She did not believe nor recognize any danger, because she may have talked to the serpent before that incident. I do not believe she knew it was Satan who was talking to her at that time.

In the book of Revelation we read about frogs coming out of the mouth of the dragon, which represents evil spirits:

> And I saw three unclean spirits like frogs coming out of the mouth of the dragon, out of the mouth of the beast, and out of the mouth of the false prophet.
>
> For they are spirits of demons, performing signs, which go out to the kings of the earth and of the whole world, to gather them to the battle of that great day of God Almighty. – Revelation 16:13-14

Daniel saw visions about what was going to happen in future. He saw nations and rulers of those nations who looked like different animals. Those animals represented the character and the particular spirit that was going to control those kings and leaders of those nations (Daniel 7-8).

Based on the Scriptures above, I believe that the reason why God separated the clean and unclean animals is based on their relationship with the spirit-world. Clean animals like the lamb and ox are pictured as Jesus, and the dove as the Holy Spirit. Unclean animals and creatures are compared to evil spirits.

Jesus said in Luke 10:19 that He has given us authority to tread on serpents and scorpions and over all the power of the enemy. *Serpents* and *scorpions* represent demons (evil spirits), and we have been given authority over these.

Two unclean animals that are used in the Bible to represent evil people and spirits are dogs and pigs (Matthew 7:6; 8:31-32; Philippians 3:2; 2 Peter 2:22; Revelation 22:15).

Though the earth became without form, void, and full of darkness, the Spirit of God never forsook the earth. He hovered over the surface of the waters, protecting the earth from the evil forces which sought to further damage it.

This is because the Spirit of God knows what is in the heart of God. He searches the deep things of God (1 Corinthians 2:10). He knew that God was not yet done with this earth, and that one day He would restore and renew it once again. He would create another type of spirit-being; and this time, they would be created in His image and likeness; and would rule and reign on this earth once again. Praise God!

Why did God create Adam or the human species? If He wanted a species of beings worshiping Him in heaven, why would He create man and put him on earth?

To be honest, He had already created plenty of beings that worship Him day and night in heaven. The Bible gives us plenty of references about those beings and their worship.

God created us to regain the planet Earth and to manage it for Him.

Chapter 4
GOD AND JESUS—AS KINGS

One of the things to keep in mind, is that our God is a *Creator* and a *King*. Before He ever became a Savior or Redeemer, we know Him to be a King.

When you come to Him, come to Him as you are coming to a king. There are plenty of references in the Bible that show us God the Father and Jesus as Kings.

Our God is a King

The Bible describes God as follows:

The Lord is King forever and ever – Psalm 10:16a.

For the kingdom is the Lord's, and He rules over the nations – Psalm 22:28.

For the Lord Most High is awesome; He is a great King over all the earth – Psalm 47:2

For God is the King of all the earth; sing praises with understanding – Psalm 47:7.

He is also called the King of glory (Psalm 24:8). Here are two more references of His royalty:

> *Where is He who has been born King of the Jews? For we have seen His star in the East and have come to worship Him* – Matthew 2:2.

> *Now to the King eternal, immortal, invisible, to God who alone is wise, be honor and glory forever and ever. Amen.* – 1 Timothy 1:17.

There were many in the Old Testament who witnessed God as King on the earth throughout their lifetimes. Why don't we see this in our day? Did God cease from being a king? Let us find this out by digging a little deeper:

> *For unto us a Child is born, unto us a Son is given; and the government will be upon His shoulder. And His name will be called Wonderful, Counselor, Mighty God, Everlasting Father, Prince of Peace.*

> *Of the increase of His government and peace there will be no end, upon the throne of David and over His kingdom, to order it and establish it with judgment and justice from that time forward, even forever.*

> *The zeal of the Lord of hosts will perform this* – Isaiah 9:6-7.

When we need help, we are told to come before the throne of grace to receive the help we need. Kings have thrones.

> *Let us therefore come boldly to the throne of grace, that we may obtain mercy and find grace to help in time of need.* – Hebrews 4:16

The verses above describe one of the most famous prophecies about our Lord Jesus Christ. The first thing it says about Him, is that the government will be upon His shoulder.

CHAPTER 4 | GOD AND JESUS—AS KINGS

How does government rest upon His shoulders?

He is the head of the church and we are His body on this earth. The shoulder is part of the body, which means the government of this earth is supposed to be on the shoulders of the church.

For some reason, we made this verse part of our eschatology, meaning something that is going to take place somewhere out there in the future. This is not true according to the verse above. Rather, that is what religion does. It steals from us what we should have now and gives us a false hope that someday things are going to be better. But faith says, "Now!"

From the phrase, "from that time forward, even forever," we understand that the fulfillment of that particular prophecy began from the time a Son was given. It says that of the increase of His government and peace, there will be no end.

This means that it *is eternal*. We all know the *Son* spoken of here is Jesus. He came two thousand years ago, and He is going to order His government with judgment and justice from that time forward, even forevermore.

This literally began two thousand years ago, but we have yet to grasp what it really means. Below are the verses from the New Testament which prove its fulfillment:

> *He will be great, and will be called the Son of the Highest; and the Lord God will give Him the throne of His father David. And He will reign over the house of Jacob forever, and of His kingdom there will be no end* – Luke 1:32-33.

The verses above are the announcement by an angel about the birth of Jesus to Mary.

When the wise men from the East came to see Jesus they came looking for the King who was born in Bethlehem. How did they receive the revelation that Jesus was a king? It was because of His star which they saw in the East (Matthew 2:2).

When He died, He died as a king also. The inscription on the cross was 'King of the Jews.' When the governor asked Jesus if He was the King of the Jews, He did not deny it. He said, "It is as you say" (Matthew 27:11).

How do we witness to others of Jesus as a king?

Believers need to be involved in the political arena of their nations. We have been avoiding politics for far too long. Because of that, the unrighteous have taken over governments all over the world. There is no righteous justice system in the world anymore. People with money make their own rules. Any wicked person with money can do almost anything anywhere in the world.

Isaiah said the government shall be upon the shoulders of Jesus (Isaiah 9:6), not on the shoulders of the devil.

Thus, church leaders should encourage believers to get involved in politics, both locally and in the central government of their nations. Otherwise, how do we witness to others that Jesus is a King?

We do not witness for Him after we die or later in eternity. We are called to be His witnesses on this earth right now.

One of the main reasons this world is in chaos is because there are not very many people witnessing about Jesus as a King. "When *the righteous are in authority,* the people rejoice: but when the wicked beareth rule, the people mourn" – Proverbs 29:2 KJV.

We have had enough mourning and groaning going on for the longest time because the righteous have been avoiding politics and government for all this time. It is time for change.

CHAPTER 4 | GOD AND JESUS—AS KINGS

Anytime I meet someone from any country, they are always complaining about how bad the government in their nation is doing and they speak against the leaders of their nations. Just talking negatively about your government is not going to change anything for the better!

The only way to change anything, is if we have witnesses for Jesus in those governments. We need believers in positions of influence for the kingdom causes that we are striving for. We must find out why we do not have any influence in government and come up with a solution.

One of the popular messages of the last few years was telling Americans to go back to their roots; that message is dying out as I write this book. America cannot go back to her roots. We need a brand new strategy.

There were fifty-six men who signed the *Declaration of Independence*. Out of the fifty-six, fifty-four of them were known to be Christians and attended some form of church. That meant their moral and ethical value system was based on Judeo-Christian ethics. That is why this country was established the way it was.

How many people do we have in our government *now* who are a witness for Jesus?

If we are going to take this country back, we need believers in positions of government—at both the state and national levels—who will witness to Jesus as a king.

Again, we are not here to take over governments; but rather, like Joseph and Daniel did, we need to have people witnessing in high places. Everyone God used in the Old Testament is a type of Christ: Moses, Joseph, David, Daniel, and Esther.

Every single person God used, manifested Christ through their life and His mission on earth. We have received the real deal, and today there are fewer witnesses for Jesus than ever in world governments.

God has anointed many people with His power to be a witness in government, but they have avoided it, thinking it is not God's will for them. The enemy has deceived us to keep us out of this most important aspect of our nation so that he can have free reign without any hindrance.

Every government on earth belongs to Jesus, because there is no authority, natural or spiritual, except His. Why should we give the authority God gave us to the devil, and then complain about what he is doing with it?

Paul calls people in governmental authority "ministers." Did you know that? In Romans chapter thirteen, he mentioned this twice. I was really surprised when I read this:

> *For he is the minister of God to thee for good*
> – Romans 13:4a KJV.

> *For this cause pay ye tribute also: for they are God's ministers, attending continually upon this very thing*
> – Romans 13:6 KJV.

I am a minister of the gospel. I preach the gospel to groups of people.

You can be in charge of the finance in the government of your nation and you are also a minister of God. You preach the gospel through your influence, your input, and your decisions. The same Holy Spirit is working through us, but in different manifestations.

Each believer is anointed to manifest at least one aspect of Jesus. When we all come together as a Body, we have the fullness of God (Ephesians 4:13).

Church, this has to happen! It must happen if Jesus is going to return to the earth. He is not coming for a church crying and whining like a baby to get them out of the earth. He is coming for a victorious church.

CHAPTER 4 | GOD AND JESUS—AS KINGS

Every person God used in the Old Testament was a type or shadow of Christ, so that means they were representing or foreshadowing Christ Who was to come.

Abraham was a prophet, Joseph was a prime minister, and David was a king. Esther was a queen, Moses was a deliverer, and the list goes on. They were all witnesses of the Messiah. Jesus is all of them, and more.

Jesus said every Scripture testifies of Him:

> *You search the Scriptures, for in them you think you have eternal life; and these are they which testify of Me* – John 5:39.

Nowhere in the Bible do we read that Jesus' reign or kingdom comes only during the millennium, or that His kingship starts once this current world system ends. That is yet another misunderstanding the deceiver brought to the church.

His physical kingdom and reign will be here on the earth only in the millennium, but He is a King forever and ever, and His kingdom is from generation to generation. Throughout the Bible it says God and Jesus' reign is for *now* and *forever*.

Old Testament Revelation

In the Old Testament, a heathen king who lived more than four-thousand years ago had a powerful revelation about the kingdom of our God, which I pray the church will get a hold of at least now.

The church keeps preaching that the kingdom of our God is going to come at some point in the future that nobody knows. Please read what this king says in the following verse:

> *And at the end of the time I, Nebuchadnezzar, lifted my eyes to heaven, and my understanding returned to me; and I*

> *blessed the Most High and praised and honored Him who lives forever: For His dominion is an everlasting dominion, And His kingdom is from generation to generation* – Daniel 4:34.

The verse above says that when his understanding was returned to the king, he had a revelation about God's kingdom Whose dominion is an everlasting dominion and His kingdom is from generation to generation. So, it is not just during the millennium.

I think that when their understanding comes back to believers worldwide, they will come to the same realization. But wait, there's more:

> *Then to Him was given dominion and glory and a kingdom, that all peoples, nations, and languages should serve Him. His dominion is an everlasting dominion, which shall not pass away, And His kingdom the one which shall not be destroyed* – Daniel 7:14.

> *To make known to the sons of men His mighty acts, and the glorious majesty of His kingdom. Your kingdom is an everlasting kingdom, and Your dominion endures throughout all generations* – Psalm 145:12-13.

You may say, "Brother, that is Old Testament. Show me some verses in the New Testament that say Jesus' kingdom and reign is for now and forever." I am glad you asked that. Below are some verses from the New Testament.

New Testament Scriptures

The revelation of the kingdom according to New Testament sources includes the following:

> *He will be great, and will be called the Son of the Highest; and the Lord God will give Him the throne of His father*

CHAPTER 4 | GOD AND JESUS—AS KINGS

David. And He will reign over the house of Jacob forever, and of His kingdom there will be no end – Luke 1:32-33.

If anyone speaks, let him speak as the oracles of God. If anyone ministers, let him do it as with the ability which God supplies, that in all things God may be glorified through Jesus Christ, to whom belong the glory and the dominion forever and ever. Amen – 1 Peter 4:11.

To Him be the glory and the dominion forever and ever. Amen – 1 Peter 5:11.

To God our Savior, who alone is wise, be glory and majesty, dominion and power, both now and forever. Amen – Jude 1:25.

And from Jesus Christ, the faithful witness, the firstborn from the dead, and the ruler over the kings of the earth. To Him who loved us and washed us from our sins in His own blood, and has made us kings and priests to His God and Father, to Him be glory and dominion forever and ever. Amen –Revelation 1:5-6.

All the verses above tell us that Jesus' kingdom and dominion is everlasting. It was here before we were born and it will be here after we die.

Chapter 5
BELIEVERS AS KINGS AND QUEENS

In every nation, people are unhappy with their governments. Failed governments and collapsing economic systems are the talk of our time.

Whenever God decides to redeem or restore a nation He raises up a king. The destiny of a nation depends on its kings.

God has only three ministry gifts; *kings, prophets*, and *priests*. Kings govern, while prophets sustain and restore the relationship between God and people, and priests do ministry among and on behalf of the people.

When God wants to restore a people to Himself, He raises up a prophet. When He wants to restore or build a nation, He raises up a king. When He wants to restore the spiritual life of a people, He raises up a priest.

Even if you have many prophets and priests in a nation, if you do not have a king or if the king is wicked, that nation will perish because a king or kings decide which direction a nation goes. This is why the role of kings is so critical.

When we study the Bible we see that whenever God wants to reveal the future of a nation and the world, He puts a dream in the heart of a king.

In Genesis we read that God gave Pharaoh a dream, but he did not understand what the dream meant. Even though Pharaoh was an evil king, God gave him that dream. So he had to call a prophet, Joseph, to interpret that dream for him.

We see in the book of Daniel that God gave a dream to Nebuchadnezzar. It may be the most important dream anyone has ever had. Again, the king could not understand the meaning of it, so he had to call in a prophet. Daniel interpreted the dream for him. The dream contained everything that was going to happen from that time until the end of the world.

God promised Abraham that kings would come out of his loins. Who are those kings? While it is true that the kings of Israel were part of this, we too are seed of Abraham by faith in Christ. The New Testament clearly teaches that we have been made kings and priests by Jesus.

Man's eternal purpose is to reign on earth. We have been taught for many years that we were created to worship God, so it is difficult for us to understand and receive the doctrine of the kingship of a believer. It's almost like we do not feel comfortable when we hear such terms, or the enemy will make us feel that we are getting into error or wrong doctrine somehow.

We have been conditioned or programmed by religious spirits, and as long as those strongholds remain in our minds we will reject the truth of what the Word says, that we are now kings and queens in the kingdom of our Lord Jesus Christ.

Imagine meeting Adam, the first man on earth, in the garden of Eden, and you ask him, "Adam, what is your purpose? Why did God create you?" What do you think his response would be?

He would tell you that God created him to have dominion over the earth. God told him to be "fruitful and multiply; fill the earth and subdue it; have dominion" (Genesis 1:28).

Would you expect him to say, "God created me to sing to Him. See that guitar out there hanging on that apple tree? He gave that to me because I am supposed to play and sing day and night." What do you think his reply would be?

If we ask Abraham, the father our faith, what his purpose was, what would he say? I believe he would say, "I am blessed to be a blessing to all the families of the earth." That's the kind of faith we inherited.

What if we ask David about his purpose? He would say, "I am a king of Israel and my throne endures forever, and I am a psalmist."

What would Adam and his descendants be doing on earth now if he had not fallen? They would be exercising dominion on the earth, the same thing he did in the beginning in the garden. That is exactly what we are supposed to be doing now. That is what the people of Israel did when they were not even saved by the blood of Jesus. How much more should we be exercising dominion now on this earth?

As long as the enemy can keep us convinced that we are not kings, he will continue to reign on earth, stealing and using all of the resources God gave to us.

When we read the Bible from Genesis to Revelation, it consistently says the same thing about mankind—that we were created by God to reign on earth (Genesis 1:26; Revelation 22:5).

As I was writing this, the Lord brought the story of elephants in India to my mind:

> If you visit to India, you will see this strange sight of huge elephants walking down the road being led by a man.

The man carries stick in his hand with a sharp knife on its end. The elephant will be carrying some coconut leaves or a load of something else between its tusks.

When the man tells the elephant to turn left, it will turn left; and when the man says to turn right, it will turn right. When he gives an order to pick something up, the elephant will pick it up, and do everything the man says.

Compared to that man, the elephant is a huge animal—the largest on earth! The man is maybe five feet tall, a skinny guy. The elephant is more than ten feet tall and weighs thousands of pounds.

Why and how does this huge animal obey a little skinny man who weighs only a fraction of its own mass?

It happens through mental conditioning or reprogramming.

The interesting thing we need to understand is how they train the elephants to be domesticated:

These elephants once lived in the wild and roamed freely. People would set up traps for the elephants along their paths, and they would fall into a deep ditch. Once the elephant falls into it, it cannot get out of it on its own.

They bring huge trucks or other elephants that have been trained to pull it out of the ditch, and place it into an iron cage.

The elephant will remain in a cage for days, as long it takes for that creature to no longer be a danger to the people and property around it.

For days and months they will torture this elephant. Every time this elephant tries to react or attack, they will pierce its body with a sharp knife or beat it with a rod.

CHAPTER 5 | BELIEVERS AS KINGS AND QUEENS

Eventually, because of the pain, the elephant begins to listen to the orders the man gives. Once it has been conditioned mentally and is no longer wild, they will bring it outside of the cage, but tie it to a tree with a chain on its legs.

It will have limited freedom to roam around the tree to the distance that the chain allows. Then the next phase of training begins.

The man will feed it, take care of it, and give it a bath. Eventually the elephant becomes friendly.

People use these elephants for temple celebrations and for doing work. It is also one of the gods the people of India worship.

We were created to reign on earth; we are kings. But, like the elephant, we fell into a trap of the enemy, the ditch of sin that was set up by the devil.

The first man that God created fell into that trap. Ever since then, we inherited a preconditioned mindset that was programed by sin and by the devil, not our original mindset. Our original mindset is the mind of Christ.

The enemy deceived us and stole the earth from us, and now he is using it to do his will. Millions of men and women who have become pawns in his hands are doing his bidding as well.

When someone becomes free from this conditioning and programming and tells others who we were originally, they will look at that person like they don't understand what they are talking about. "What are you trying to say? You want me to reign in life? I am worried about how I'm going to pay my next car payment or rent for my apartment."

Where do these types of thoughts come from? From years of conditioning we have inherited from our parents, culture, and society.

Church people can watch and make movies, start all kinds of businesses, drink wine, be involved in sports, start schools and hospitals, go to parties, and do almost everything else in a society;, but the moment you tell them they need to become the mayor of their city or be part of the city council, or involved in politics, they will get a strange look on their face, like a deer caught in headlights. They will resist and come up with all kinds of excuses, saying, "No, that's not for us now, only when Jesus comes." What stupidity is that?

It's time for us to get free from the programming that happened through sin and by our enemy, and receive everything the Lord has for us.

Both the Old and New Testaments call us a royal priesthood (Exodus 19:6; 1 Peter 2:9). There has been much teaching on the priesthood of a believer, but not much (almost none) on the royalty and kingship of a believer. Because of that, we have so many believers who sing and pray, but few who know how to rule.

We have so many Bible schools and seminaries that train people how to become a priest or a minister, but almost none that train believers to become kings!

Though God entrusted the whole earth to us, most people live and act like paupers, and do not live a life worth living. They are waiting to leave this earth. What a sad dilemma!

They teach that every believer is a priest unto God. For some reason, they forgot what the rest of the same verse says; or, for that matter, what the first part of that verse says.

It talks about the royalty, or the kingship, of a believer. If every believer is a priest according to that verse, ladies and gentlemen, let me correct that teaching and re-establish something biblical here, by saying, "Every believer is a king."

If nations are to be restored to God, the kings in those nations must be released. When the Bible says that Jesus has made us kings and priests unto God, it does not say some are priests and others are kings. It means *every* believer is a king and a priest at the same time.

We are not conformed after the saints in the Old Testament. When we are Born Again, we are recreated into the image of Jesus Christ, Who is a King, a Prophet, and a Priest— all at the same time.

Man Was Created to Have Dominion over the Earth

From the very outset, it is forever recorded:

> *Then God said, 'Let Us make man in Our image, according to Our likeness; let them have dominion over the fish of the sea, over the birds of the air, and over the cattle, over all the earth and over every creeping thing that creeps on the earth.'*
>
> *So God created man in His own image; in the image of God He created him; male and female He created them.*
>
> *Then God blessed them, and God said to them, 'Be fruitful and multiply; fill the earth and subdue it; have dominion over the fish of the sea, over the birds of the air, and over every living thing that moves on the earth'* – Genesis 1:26-28.

In the verses above, God the Creator mentions the purpose for creating man: That is, to have dominion on earth.

Only the manufacturer knows the purpose of a product. It is very important that we understand this. We all have preconceived notions in our hearts and minds that were taught by the religious spirit about our purpose. So, when we read the above Scripture, we assume we know it;, but truthfully, very few people on this earth fully understand its meaning.

The word *dominion* is not a common word. It's a king-dom word. Dominion is the influence of a kingdom over a territory. Kingdoms have dominion. And kings have kingdoms (king, kingdom, and dominion).

As I mentioned earlier, God was extending the dominion of His kingdom to earth, and He created man to exercise that dominion. Or, He exercises His dominion through man.

We need to root out what has been taught by the religious spirit and replace it with the above truth.

In order to understand our individual purpose, we need to understand why God created the human race.

The verses above tell us how and why God created us. We are created in the image and likeness of God to have dominion over the earth.

Each one of us is created to have dominion over a particular area of life, and God has equipped each human being with the capacity and ability to do this. This could be a purpose, dream, vision, product, or calling.

He deposited our purpose in us in seed form. When we discover that seed and follow the principles or the steps he laid out in verse twenty-eight above,, we will prosper.

There is no one born on this earth without this seed. The problem is, many have simply not discovered it yet. We also call the seed "potential" or "talent." Each seed needs a particular environment in order to grow and be fruitful.

Man's eternal purpose is to be a king on this earth. Kings have kingdoms, and kingdoms have dominion. Adam was a king, and at the end there will only be kings like it was in the beginning.

However, because of the fall, God added two additional dimensions to man's life, which are to be a priest and a prophet. These two dimensions are temporary, until such time as we are redeemed from this present life. Once we are redeemed, we will reign on the new earth once again, forever and ever (Revelation 5:10; 22:5).

As I mentioned, there is a teaching in the body of Christ that says you are either a king or a priest. People who are in ministry are called priests and people who work in the secular world or run a business are called kings. However, the New Testament does not advocate this line of teaching.

Christ is a King, Priest, and Prophet—all at the same time. Each believer is also supposed to function in all of these dimensions.

Abraham, David, and other Old Testament saints, who lived in the revelation of life in Jesus, functioned in all of these three roles. The Hebrew word for dominion is *Radah*, which means "to rule, have dominion, dominate, tread down."[17]

When I first learned that Jesus is the King of kings, I thought He was the King of all the kings in all kingdoms that ruled the earth before. However, God opened my eyes to see that it was talking about Him being the King of us who have been made kings and priests by His Father.

From Genesis to Revelation, it is God's plan to establish His kingdom on this earth as it is in heaven, and for man to have dominion over the works of His hands. God is a king and we are His children. Whatever He does from Genesis to Revelation has a kingdom flavor.

Kings rule over a territory, and that territory is called a kingdom. This is why whenever God mentions the position of man, He always

---

17 Strong's Hebrew Lexicon

puts the kingship first, and not the priesthood. Please read the verses below and you will see what I am talking about.

Right now, everyone in the body of Christ is a king and priest at the same time. When God brought the people of Israel out of Egypt, He said He wanted them to be a kingdom of priests:

> *'And you shall be to Me a kingdom of priests and a holy nation.' These are the words which you shall speak to the children of Israel* – Exodus 19:6.

We see the same thing in the New Testament:

> *But you are a chosen generation, a royal priesthood, a holy nation, His own special people, that you may proclaim the praises of Him who called you out of darkness into His marvelous light* –1 Peter 2:9.

> *And from Jesus Christ, the faithful witness, the firstborn from the dead, and the ruler over the kings of the earth. To Him who loved us and washed us from our sins in His own blood, and has made us kings and priests to His God and Father, to Him be glory and dominion forever and ever. Amen* – Revelation 1:5-6.

> *And have made us kings and priests to our God; and we shall reign on the earth* – Revelation 5:10.

> *There will never be night again. They will not need the light of a lamp or the light of the sun, because the Lord God will give them light. And they will rule as kings forever and ever* – Revelation 22:5 NCV.

None of the Scriptures above say that God made some kings and others priests. Instead, they say He made us kings *and* priests. That includes everyone. Revelation 22 mentions only kings. That is the finale. Amen.

God wants each of us to exercise our royalty *first* before we move into any other capacity that He created us for. Royalty is your identity, and when you exercise your kingship (dominion) over an area of life, you will have provision for living.

Jesus is a King, Prophet, and Priest. When the wise men from the East came to see Him, they came to see a king, not a prophet or a priest (Matthew 2:1). During His ministry time on earth, He functioned as a Prophet and a Priest, and not as a King.

At His death, He was once again recognized as a King. When He comes back the second time, He is coming as a King. Not just any king, but as the King of kings.

The enemy knows that if he can keep us busy singing songs inside a building, we will not bother him with the dominion of the earth. We will stay inside our homes and church buildings, singing songs.

God did not ask Adam to sing to Him. He did not give Adam a guitar or a violin and tell him to sit in the garden and sing to Him on the seventh day!

Throughout the Bible, God says we are created to reign on this earth. What if a cow stays in its stall and sings all day long? Will it fulfill its purpose? No.

A fig tree is created to produce figs. When Jesus saw a fig tree and it did not have any fruit, He cursed it. He did not say, "Well, at least it is praising me, so let it remain fruitless." He said that no one would eat fruit from it ever again (Mark 11:14).

David had a passion for worship, but his primary purpose was to be a king. We make songs and sing about him and how he danced before the Lord. Well, let us not only dance like David danced, but reign like David reigned! It is easy to dance, but not so easy to reign. To reign, you need to discover your purpose and master at least one area of life.

Another big deception the enemy has used, is to make people believe that God created us to live in heaven. I do not see that anywhere in the book of Genesis or in the book of Revelation—or anywhere in between.

The devil knows that if he can keep us ignorant of the fact that the earth belongs to us, then he can freely misuse the whole earth and its resources for his purpose, and man will not bother him.

God created mankind to live on this earth, and gave him the earth to manage. We are going to reign with Christ on the *new earth*, not in heaven. But we will only know how to reign with Him in the next life if we learn how to reign in this life.

There were more people who were called to influence or engage in government in the Old Testament than in any other area. But today, there are less people who are influencing or engaged with government.

As I said, those who are called to be in government now are sitting in the pews of some church, frustrated and angry about what is going on in their country. They know in their heart they are called to do something with the government, but they do not know exactly what to do, because they have never been taught about it. That is the reason for most of the turmoil going on in the nations.

Blessing and Anointing of the Firstborn

In the Bible, a firstborn son carried a different right and anointing than the rest. He received a double-portion inheritance together with the authority to represent the father in all business transactions and before kings and governments.

The firstborn is like the king of the entire household, and the younger brothers have to submit to him and his authority. Eventually, they became the elders of the land.

CHAPTER 5 | BELIEVERS AS KINGS AND QUEENS

Also I will make him My firstborn, the highest of the kings of the earth – Psalm 89:27.

Adam was the firstborn of all humans. The Bible says, "God blessed them" (Adam and Eve in Genesis 1:28). What blessing did God give them?

They were already blessed; they were living in a perfect environment and were blessed with every blessing we can imagine. Why did they need to be blessed again? The blessing God gave them was the blessing of the firstborn; to be the king and queen and judge of the whole earth. Those are our great-grandparents, and we are supposed to be following in their footsteps. God has not changed His mind concerning humanity just because Adam fell.

Where and how did the patriarchs of our faith learn to bless their children and their firstborn? They learned it from their God, Elohim. If you study the blessings our forefathers gave to their children in Genesis, we see they followed the same pattern and wording God used in Genesis chapter one when they blessed their children. People like Isaac, Jacob, and Joseph, when they blessed their children, told them to "be fruitful" (Genesis 28:3).

The word *fruitful* appears thirteen times in the book of Genesis. Out of the thirteen times, for the majority of these, God was saying it to bless His people.

Keep in mind that, in those days and times, people mostly lived as tribes; and the more people there were in a tribe, the more influence and power the head of the tribe had in the land:.

In a multitude of people is a king's honor, but in the lack of people is the downfall of a prince – Proverbs 14:28.

When you are not blessed as the firstborn, you struggle to survive by making the bare minimum. When you are blessed, what others struggle for comes easy for you. The Bible says, "The blessing of the Lord makes one rich, and He adds no sorrow with it" (Proverbs 10:22).

The reason why God was pleased with the sacrifice of Abel was because he brought the firstborn of his flock and their fat. That means he gave God the best of what he had (Genesis 4:4).

Why am I sharing about the blessing of the firstborn in a book dedicated to kings and queens?

When someone is Born Again, they become a firstborn in the family of God. They are re-entitled to receive the blessings, favor, and the inheritance of a firstborn.

Many believers struggle almost all their lives and never get ahead, while some children of the wicked one buys up the whole neighborhood or starts the next successful business. We wonder why they prosper. It's because of the blessing.

When the firstborn disobeys or is disqualified because he does not exercise his position, then it will pass on to whomever the father, or God, chooses. There are many examples like that in the Bible.

Joseph is an example of one who received the blessing of the firstborn. Though he was the eleventh child, he received the right to be a firstborn in the spirit. Being a firstborn has more to do with position and authority, than birth order.

Another example is Esau, who sold his firstborn birthright to his younger brother, Jacob, for a cup of stew. Despite it being God's election based on His foreknowledge that Esau was going to make that choice in his life, He chose Jacob to receive the blessing from their father.

In the New Testament, everyone Born Again through Jesus Christ is a *firstborn*. Because Jesus is the firstborn from the dead, everyone born

CHAPTER 5 | BELIEVERS AS KINGS AND QUEENS

after Him inherits the same blessing and authority. There is no second born in Christ's family. Every believer receives the authority and inheritance of the firstborn (Romans 8:29; Colossians 1:8; Hebrews 12:23).

Imagine you are the firstborn in a rich family, and after your father dies, you receive the double-portion of the blessings everyone else receives.

Now, imagine you are born into God's family, the richest person in the universe. How much authority and inheritance should you receive?

We have received an inheritance (Ephesians 1:11). That is why the Bible says we are co-heirs with Jesus Christ.

When David's time came to appoint a successor for his throne, there was confusion in the family because he had so many firstborn through several different women. They all began to fight for the throne; and some of them went ahead and self-appointed themselves as kings. Despite that, God chose Solomon to be David's successor.

But a firstborn son, as long as he is a child, is not better than a servant (Galatians 4:1-5). They have to mature in their understanding of who they really are and what God has given them.

There are many in the body of Christ who have no idea who they are and what God has given them. They live based on the inheritance, culture, and background of their natural father. Unless a person receives the revelation and takes it by force, this blessing will not come to them.

Chapter 6
THE RESPONSIBILITIES OF A KING

Though we are called and created as kings by our God, we are not all created to be presidents and prime ministers of nations. That is quite impossible.

The responsibilities of a king are divided into ten areas of operation. Each believer is called and destined to be involved in one or more areas of these ten categories. I will explain each of them below.

As you read, please be open to the voice of the Holy Spirit to hear which area you are called to influence. As a king or a queen, you are created to exercise your gift and talent in one of these areas in your nation, and to have dominion over that area.

1. Political Government

The first area a king needs to exercise his dominion in is government. There is a common understanding or meaning that comes with the noun *king* in any language or culture of this earth. That is one who rules or is in authority. That is the number one responsibility of a king, to govern. He is in the office of government.

Adam was the first king on this earth because he was created to reign on this earth. Jesus, the Last Adam, will be the last King and the King who reigns forever. If Adam (the first man) was a king, everyone born after him would naturally be a king as well.

There are believers who are called to be presidents and prime ministers of nations. We have to teach and train our people about this. There are believers who are called to be governors or ministers of states, city mayors, council members, county clerks, and village officers.

We should be purposefully training our people to be in places of influence.

Paul calls people who are government, leaders or rulers, "ministers of God" in his epistle to the Romans:

> For rulers are not a terror to good works, but to evil. Do you want to be unafraid of the authority? Do what is good, and you will have praise from the same. For he is God's minister to you for good – Romans 13:3-4a.

> For because of this you also pay taxes, for they are God's ministers attending continually to this very thing. Render therefore to all their due: taxes to whom taxes are due, customs to whom customs, fear to whom fear, honor to whom honor – Romans 13:6-7.

What a sad situation it is with the current generation, who have been trained only to have fun and pleasure, and are addicted to the things of Lucifer, and are bewitched by what he produces. They want everything for free, and do not like to pay any price. They cannot see anything beyond what their natural eyes can see. Every morning they wake up thinking about what they are going to do to have fun. How much sugar and junk food can I eat today? Which movie is being released? Which sports team is winning or losing? That's the talk they spend their majority of their time on.

Kings don't think like that. When kings come together or have a council meeting with their elders, they are thinking about how they can expand their territory; which new horizon they are going to conquer, what they are going to do to develop the land God gave them, and how they can train the younger ones to reach new heights. That's how kings think.

Government is the major area of God's interest. Because He is a King and has a kingdom, He understands and is more passionate about it than we are. This is why He used more people in government to influence government in the Bible.

There are different branches of government and political offices. If you are called to the government as a king, you are called to be involved in one of those offices at some level.

2. Land

Once you understand the kingdom of God and your responsibility in His kingdom, the first thing you realize is your connection with the land.

If you have no revelation of the land and you do not feel any connection with the land you live in, then you do not have a real revelation of God or His kingdom.

To a king, the extent of his landholdings and people determine his kingdom. The size of the land shows the size of his kingdom. If there is no land, there is no kingdom.

If an enemy has taken over the land, then that king loses his kingdom. This is what happened to this earth. The enemy has taken over the land from us.

Even today, when false religious groups enter a new region, the first thing they do is buy a prime piece of land to establish their center. They will not have a crusade or food distribution first. They will establish a center, and then they will start doing community works. I have heard that the Mormon Church owns the largest amount of land next to the US government west of the Mississippi River in the USA.

The Bible says the earth and its fullness belong to the Lord (Psalm 24:1). At the same time, it says that if God's people humble themselves and pray and forsake their sins, then God will heal their land. Why does the land need to be healed?

The land was cursed because of the fall of man and thus the earth lost its power to produce to its full capacity. It stopped yielding its strength. Instead, it began to produce thorns and thistles.

Sin and the shedding of innocent blood corrupted the land. If the land is to yield its strength again, we need to redeem the land.

God wants you to be a landowner

Again, the devil will try his best to keep believers from owning any land. The biggest fight you will fight in your life will be to possess a piece of land. The first thing you need to do as a king and an heir of God on this earth is own a piece of land in your own name.

It is the responsibility of each believer to possess a piece of land and invite King Jesus to come and rule over that property and to release that property to Him, for Him to use it to reign in that region. This is not a "me, mine, and I" philosophy. These are kingdom principles I am teaching you.

Once you own the land, it's up to the King to tell you what to do on it or with it. Sometimes He will tell you to give it away to someone

CHAPTER 6 | THE RESPONSIBILITIES OF A KING

who doesn't have any land. He may tell you to establish a business, ministry, school, nursing home, or to use it for agriculture. A farmer who is a believer and owns land and does agriculture, is a king.

When Jesus shared parables about the kingdom of God, He shared about buying and owning land because there is treasure of the kingdom of heaven hidden in the land, which few understand.

Everything you are and have is connected to land. Everything we eat and use comes from the land. No land, no kingdom; no kingdom, no dominion.

> *Again, the kingdom of heaven is like treasure hidden in a field, which a man found and hid; and for joy over it he goes and sells all that he has and buys that field* – Matthew 13:44.

I was surprised by the parable above. The man did not sell everything he had to buy the treasure, but to buy the land because the treasure was hidden in the field.

What was the treasure hidden in the field? It was the kingdom of heaven:

> *For the kingdom of heaven is like a landowner who went out early in the morning to hire laborers for his vineyard* – Matthew 20:1.

. God is the King of all the earth (Psalm 47:2). What is the Earth? The physical planet. Why is God the King of all the earth? Because you need land to exercise dominion.

Every call and covenant of God is connected to land. It is our responsibility as the children of God to redeem and heal the land so that it will yield its strength once again to produce food to eliminate hunger from the face of the earth.

There is land in nations that is lying vacant and desolate. As kingdom representatives, we are supposed to move into those regions to make those wildernesses into a garden of life:

> *I will open rivers in desolate heights, and fountains in the midst of the valleys; I will make the wilderness a pool of water, and the dry land springs of water* – Isaiah 41:18.

> *Behold, I will do a new thing, now it shall spring forth; shall you not know it? I will even make a road in the wilderness and rivers in the desert* –Isaiah 43:19.

> *For the Lord will comfort Zion, He will comfort all her waste places; He will make her wilderness like Eden, and her desert like the garden of the Lord; joy and gladness will be found in it, thanksgiving and the voice of melody* – Isaiah 51:3.

Less than ten percent of the landmass of earth is inhabited. As kings, we need to move into those vast areas of land and build new self-sustaining communities. People complain about the trouble and pollution in cities.

Why can't we be like the patriarchs who established nations? As God's children, we are supposed to possess it and make it like the garden of Eden for the benefit of humanity.

> *Because of the transgression of a land, many are its princes; but by a man of understanding and knowledge right will be prolonged* – Proverbs 28:2.

The verse above is powerful. One of the problems in third-world countries is division in governments, families, and churches. The verse above gives the clue to the reason for this. Because of the transgression of a land, many are its princes.

CHAPTER 6 | THE RESPONSIBILITIES OF A KING

Though we are all kings, we are not all called to be leaders of nations. As kings, each of us is called to one of the ten areas mentioned in this book.

When there is so much transgression that has been done in the land, there is no way people can be united to achieve a goal. There will not be any unity.

The same thing is happening in the United States these days. There is so much violence in our cities, young people are protesting and destroying public property. These young people do not know their purpose, and so, they are wandering in the streets.

There is no unity in the government or between communities, and so much transgression has been done to the land and in the land, that now the land is refusing to submit. This is another reason for the increase in natural calamities in this nation as well:

> *Do not defile yourselves with any of these things; for by all these the nations are defiled, which I am casting out before you.*
>
> *For the land is defiled; therefore I visit the punishment of its iniquity upon it, and the land vomits out its inhabitants.*
>
> *You shall therefore keep My statutes and My judgments, and shall not commit any of these abominations, either any of your own nation or any stranger who dwells among you (for all these abominations the men of the land have done, who were before you, and thus the land is defiled), lest the land vomit you out also when you defile it, as it vomited out the nations that were before you* – Leviticus 18:24-28.

How can the land vomit out its inhabitants?

Land is not a person or living creature. However, the land has much more sensitivity than most people think or understand. The earth will itself testify of all of the wickedness that has been done on it. Moses said he called heaven and earth to be a witness against God's people:

> *I call heaven and earth to witness against you this day, that you will soon utterly perish from the land which you cross over the Jordan to possess; you will not prolong your days in it, but will be utterly destroyed* – Deuteronomy 4:26.

The land can mourn because of the sins of its inhabitants (Isaiah 24:4-6; Jeremiah 4:28; 12:4; Hosea 4:3). When you buy a piece of land, make sure you redeem it from every curse that has been operating in it. Please "ask" its forgiveness for all the atrocities done on it. There are resources you can look up that will help you do this.

3. Administer Justice, Judgment, and Righteousness

Here's what the Word of God declares in this regard:

> *A king who sits on the throne of judgment scatters all evil with his eyes* – Proverbs 20:8.

> *The king establishes the land by justice, but he who receives bribes overthrows it* –Proverbs 29:4.

> *The king who judges the poor with truth, his throne will be established forever* – Proverbs 29:14.

> *Take away the wicked from before the king, and his throne will be established in righteousness* – Proverbs 25:5.

There are kings who are called to be judges in our nations. In the US people are in uproar when their presidents appoint Supreme Court judges, depending on their moral leniency. The judges uphold and defend the laws of the land. They define and defend the constitution.

CHAPTER 6 | THE RESPONSIBILITIES OF A KING

What they decide becomes the final law of the land. They are kings of the land.

Jesus is a Judge. We need people witnessing for Jesus as Judge in our nations. In 2 Timothy 4:8, Paul said:

> *Finally, there is laid up for me the crown of righteousness, which the Lord, the righteous Judge, will give to me on that Day, and not to me only but also to all who have loved His appearing.*

We need righteous judges in every nation on earth. People are crying out for justice and righteousness. Corruption is a major problem worldwide.

What the church has been doing, is only talking and complaining about it for a long time. That will not make any difference nor bring about the needed changes to the situation.

What will bring the changes to the situation is when believers who are educated in that field step up and play their role, bringing the change that we dream of. Believers make lame excuses, saying the judicial and political system in their nation is too corrupt and dangerous so they cannot do anything about it.

Imagine what kind of corrupt nation Joseph, Daniel, Nehemiah, Mordecai, and Esther were living in. I do not believe our nations are more corrupt now than those nations were back then.

Imagine living in a kingdom where the king was influenced by one of his assistants and issued a decree to murder the entire Christian population. And then imagine God working to turn that situation around, and the very people who desired harm for God's people were destroyed. We have not seen such things yet in our day and time.

> *Let the heavens declare His righteousness, For God Himself is Judge. Selah* – Psalm 50:6.

> *But God is the Judge: He puts down one, and exalts another*
> — Psalm 75:7.

> *Rise up, O Judge of the earth; render punishment to the proud*
> — Psalm 94:2.

If our heavenly Father is a judge, then we are supposed to be the judges of this earth.

4. Business and Services

There has been much teaching on the subject of believers being involved in the business world. However, it limits kings' involvement to that arena, and calls it "market place ministry." This has created our current problem in this nation.

The reason why Christianity and biblical moral values are in decline in the western world is because people who are supposed to be involved in the government are sitting in our pews talking about things that have no eternal value.

There are kings who are called to be working in the business world. There is nothing wrong with believers starting and doing business. In some parts of the world, Christians believe that if you are a believer, it is a sin to be in business. This is another deception of the enemy. There were many believers, both men and women, in the New Testament who were business people. Joseph of Arimathea, Dorcas, and Lydia were just some of them.

These kings are the ones who are supposed to create wealth in order to support the work of the Lord. They need to be anointed with the power to create wealth.

If you are called to start a business, make sure you find an apostle and have him pray over you and commission you to go into the business world.

CHAPTER 6 | THE RESPONSIBILITIES OF A KING

When people go into ministry, they are always ordained or commissioned by other mature ministers. I believe we need to do that for all believers who are entering into any field of influence.

In the Bible, kings were anointed and appointed by prophets or priests. If that was needed then, it is needed right now as well.

As I mentioned earlier, the enemy will not give up his hold on the wealth of this earth without a fight. You need the spiritual authority in order to break through those strongholds. I know many believers who started businesses but these did not go anywhere, while some others who prospered had no time for the Lord. They were not able to win the fight on their own.

> *As sorrowful, yet always rejoicing; as poor, yet making many rich; as having nothing, and yet possessing all things* – 2 Corinthians 6:10.

What is Paul talking about in the verse above? How was Paul poor but at the same time he made many others rich?

First of all, Paul remained poor in natural wealth because that was his personal choice. In the spirit, however, he possessed all things and everything was at his disposal, but he did not let the things of this world have any hold on his heart.

Paul made many others rich because he had the keys to the kingdom economy. He commissioned or ordained believers in the Corinthian church to go out and make money. I believe he laid hands on and prayed over them for God to release the power upon them to create wealth.

It was to the Corinthian church that God revealed, through Paul, the secret of kingdom economy. He wrote, "For you know the grace of our Lord Jesus Christ, that though He was rich, yet for your sakes

He became poor, that you through His poverty might become rich" (2 Corinthians 8:9).

Here's the principle behind it all:

> *And you shall remember the Lord your God, for it is He who gives you power to get wealth, that He may establish His covenant which He swore to your fathers, as it is this day* – Deuteronomy 8:18.

> *You are already full! You are already rich! You have reigned as kings without us—and indeed I could wish you did reign, that we also might reign with you!* – 1 Corinthians 4:8.

Paul did not try to refute it by saying, "Oh my gosh, I can't believe you guys are reigning in Corinth, that is not for now, that's for the millennium. Rather, just continue to sing songs and wait for the rapture guys. I can't believe what you are doing!"

I am glad he did not say that. Rather, he supported the idea and wanted them to reign. I am sure it was Paul who taught them about their purpose, because he established the church in Corinth. They received his teaching and applied it to real life, and saw great results.

The Corinthian church became a rich or wealthy church in a short period of time. They reigned as kings. Wow! That's our purpose. They were not singing inside the four walls every Sunday morning. Nor were they waiting for a revival or rapture. They reigned in Corinth as kings. I hope you are hearing what the Spirit is saying to the churches.

It was to the Corinthian church that God revealed, through Paul, the secret of kingdom economy. He wrote, "For you know the grace of our Lord Jesus Christ, that though He was rich, yet for your sakes He became poor, that you through His poverty might become rich" (2 Corinthians 8:9).

5. Establish and Enforce the Law or the Judicial System

There are kings who are called to fight the current political system of their nation in order to establish a righteous legal and judicial system.

For example, in the United States there are many incidents where ordinary people went to court to fight for "justice" and the verdict subsequently became a law for everyone in the nation.

Unfortunately, many times—or should I say, most times—it was the ungodly who were fighting to establish their evil intent, and they won; and consequently, we have been paying the price for many generations.

Another group of kings who are involved in this arena are the police force or the law enforcement departments of our nation.

6. Protect and Fight for His People

In a kingdom, the king goes out to fight against its enemies. In our modern day, our presidents and prime ministers do not go out to fight wars; they just give orders.

Nevertheless, there are kings who are called to be involved in their nation's army. There are hundreds and thousands of believers who are in the armed forces in our nations. They fight to protect the nation and people. They are kings.

If you want to know what kings and kingdoms do, just look at the devil and his children and what they do. He used to be a king and still has a kingdom. He enables his children to occupy key or high places in society and influence the culture and people. Where did he learn that from? From our heavenly Father: the great King.

7. Development

There are kings who are called to the development of a nation. Any development that takes place in any area of life or study is done through kings.

Pioneers and entrepreneurs are kings. The reason why many nations remain undeveloped is because the kings in their nations are not being released to do so. They are singing in their churches about what David and Moses did.

Kings, please go out and be the kings in your country. God did not create you to sing; He created you to reign!

Heathens are not taught to sing in their religious system, so they go out and make a difference in their countries. That is why the biggest businesses and corporations are owned by unbelievers.

8. Teach His People Wisdom

Another responsibility of a king is to teach the people in their nation the wisdom, knowledge, and understanding of God. These are kings who are the teachers, orators, and authors of our time. They bring out the hidden wisdom of God so people can apply this and solve their problems.

One of Joseph's responsibilities was to teach Pharaoh's elders wisdom. That meant whenever Egypt had a problem which the elders couldn't solve, they came to Joseph to ask for wisdom and counsel:.

> *He (Pharaoh) made him lord of his house, and ruler of all his possessions, to bind his princes at his pleasure, and teach his elders wisdom* – Psalm 105:21-22.

CHAPTER 6 | THE RESPONSIBILITIES OF A KING

We read the same thing about Daniel. He was promoted to be the head of all the wise men in all of Babylon:.

> *Then the king promoted Daniel and gave him many great gifts; and he made him ruler over the whole province of Babylon, and chief administrator over all the wise men of Babylon* – Daniel 2:48.

> *There is a man in your kingdom in whom is the Spirit of the Holy God. And in the days of your father, light and understanding and wisdom, like the wisdom of the gods, were found in him; and King Nebuchadnezzar your father—your father the king—made him chief of the magicians, astrologers, Chaldeans, and soothsayers* – Daniel 5:11.

The best teachers and the wisest people in any nation should be believers, because they carry the Spirit of God in them. But I am not sure these days what spirit most believers carry. The moment they get Spirit-filled they seem to lose touch with reality and this earth. In the Bible, when people were filled with the Spirit of God they always did extraordinary things.

I wonder if the spirit many receive is a religious spirit or the spirit of this world, because most people love the things of this world more than they love God or His kingdom. They will create time for the things of the world, but they have no time for God. They wouldn't say that, but if you examine their lives and how they spend their time you will find it to be the case. There is no evidence of God in their lives in any area other than their church attendance. They live an ordinary life like any unbeliever. All they know is to sing, shout, and jump up and down. Lord, have mercy!

Paul said very clearly that it is possible for a believer in Christ to receive a spirit other than the Holy Spirit. "For if he who comes preaches another Jesus whom we have not preached, or *if* you receive a different spirit which you have not received, or a different gospel which you have not accepted—you may well put up with it!" (2 Corinthians 11:4).

In the book of Daniel, we see that when the king's training was finished, Daniel and his friends were found to be ten times better in everything than the ungodly. That was also the case with the people of Israel. They were the head and were above the heathen nations.

We have to remember that we received the same promise and are part of the same covenant God made with Israel.

The religious spirit has deceived us for far too long, and has stolen or hidden from us almost everything God has given to us. When we are free from the stronghold of religion, we will begin to see the things God has prepared for those who love Him.

When the presidents and political leaders of our nation need help or solutions to the problems our nation is facing, they should want to look to the church. They should want to call ordinary believers who are filled with the Spirit and wisdom of God, and ask for their counsel. This is what God intended for and through His church.

9. Manage the Wealth and Resources of the Earth and Nations

> It is the glory of God to conceal a matter, but the glory of kings is to search out a matter –Proverbs 25:2.

God has hidden every precious thing on this earth so that natural eyes will not find them easily. Precious metals and stones are some of these, but the greatest of all is wisdom. He hides these so only people who are very serious about them will ever find them. Kings need to search out and bring these to light so others can benefit from them.

There are many different types of resources on earth and in nations. It is impossible for me to list them all here. The most important resources are human resources. We need to help people discover their purpose and re-establish a relationship with their Creator. As a king, you are called to be part of managing resources for the establishment of God's kingdom on earth.

A king can recognize potential that is hidden in a person or on this earth. The verse above is very powerful. It is the glory of God to conceal a matter, but the glory of kings to search out a matter.

God hides things so that the kings can search these out and bring them to light. One of the ways kings manifest their glory is by revealing to the world the glory of God.

10. Recognize and Promote People who are Excelling in various Fields

It is in the very nature of a king to recognize excellence. They are always looking for people who are excelling in their work in order to appreciate and promote them.

That is why the wisest man said, "Do you see a man *who* excels in his work? He will stand before kings; he will not stand before unknown *men*" (Proverbs 22:29).

There are many incidents in the Bible where a king promoted or honored someone because they saw the wisdom of God operating through that person. Kings will always appreciate excellence, wisdom, truth, and loyalty. Joseph, Mordecai, Esther, and Daniel are some examples of people who were honored and promoted by kings.

As a king, please make sure you take time and make room to recognize and appreciate excellence in people who serve you. You should always be looking to bring out the best in everything and everyone. Kings are always looking to influence and take over new territories. They require the best of the best.

The Bible is a book of kings and kingdoms. It doesn't matter which type of government you live under, you can read God's Word and learn how a king and a kingdom operates. That's one of the reasons God gave us the Bible. The Bible talks more about kings and prophets than any other calling.

Chapter 7
THE CHARACTER AND NATURE OF A KING

As I was writing this book, the historic election results just came out in the United States. To everyone's surprise, Donald Trump won the election and he is preparing for his inauguration. But as a nation, there is wide unrest and thousands of people are protesting in the streets. They are not happy with their newly-elected president. Why?

Though he might be one of the richest presidents this nation has ever had, many are not happy with his character. Nevertheless, God appointed him to be head of this nation, maybe because he is the best He has to work with now, and will work out His purpose through him.

Just because we have a newly-elected president, this nation will not be restored to God. It will be restored when kings and queens whom God has appointed rise up from the four corners of this land and take their place. This book is intended for that purpose.

The Bible teaches a whole lot about the character of a king. There is one king in the Old Testament who was called a man after God's own heart: David. Many interpret this statement to be about David's passion to worship God. I don't believe that. I believe God said this about him because he was a *king* after God's own heart. David represented God's heart as a King to the people.

Though David made many mistakes, he is the only king who demonstrated the character and heart of God toward the people and the land he was leading and reigning over. It was during his reign, the Bible says, that the land was subdued under him. This was not said about any other king:

> *Is* not the Lord your God with you? And has He *not* given you rest on every side? For He has given the inhabitants of the land into my hand, and the land is subdued before the Lord and before His people – 1 Chronicles 22:18.

Not only that, but when David appointed singers and musicians to praise and give glory to the Lord of Israel, he had a kingdom and wealth to show to the world his God Whom he was talking about. I want you to understand this very clearly.

In today's church there is so much singing going on saying, "Lord, we give you glory, honor, riches, and power;," but, those are just empty words, and have no substance to back them up.

When we give God the glory, we should have something to show or offer to Him that brings glory to His name. Otherwise, those are mere words, and He does not receive anything out of that.

When we say we give the Lord riches, we should have some riches to bring to Him. Imagine in the natural you are coming before a king to seek his favor. You are coming to his palace to meet him. You come into the inner court where the king is seated on his throne. You are one of the many citizens of his kingdom. You come and tell the king that all the riches, glory, and power belong to him, but you don't have

CHAPTER 7 | THE CHARACTER AND NATURE OF A KING

anything to show or give to the king. I don't think he will be pleased with you, unless you are very poor.

In the olden days it was customary for people and visitors from other countries to bring gifts to present before a king when they came to see him. They brought the best of the best of whatever they possessed; otherwise the king wouldn't be pleased.

That should be the attitude we have when we come before our great King. If we do not have anything, let's go and make something to bring to Him and then come before Him. He is not interested in vain words.

The Bible says during David's time:

> *King David also dedicated these to the Lord, along with the silver and gold that he had brought from all these nations—from Edom, from Moab, from the people of Ammon, from the Philistines, and from Amalek* – 1 Chronicles 18:11.

> *Indeed I have taken much trouble to prepare for the house of the Lord one hundred thousand talents of gold and one million talents of silver, and bronze and iron beyond measure, for it is so abundant. I have prepared timber and stone also, and you may add to them* – 1 Chronicles 22:14.

The verse above gives us a glimpse into the kind of wealth David prepared for building the house of the Lord. One hundred thousand talents of gold are equal to 7,500,000 pounds of gold, and one million talents of silver are equal to 75,000,000 pounds of silver in our day. That's just gold and silver. For bronze, iron, and wood it was immeasurable. Wow! As a king, He did not amass all that wealth for himself or even for his children. He collected it for the house of the Lord, to honor his King. That is how to reach the heart of a king!

> *Now for the house of my God I have prepared with all my might: gold for things to be made of gold, silver for things*

of silver, bronze for things of bronze, iron for things of iron, wood for things of wood, onyx stones, stones to be set, glistening stones of various colors, all kinds of precious stones, and marble slabs in abundance – 1 Chronicles 29:2.

The next time we sing about David or sing the songs David wrote to God, we should think about what kind of man he was and what he accomplished with his life as a king for the Lord.

We should at least do one percent of what he did before we sing about bringing honor, glory, power, and riches due unto God's name.

I have noticed a peculiar thing about human beings. Other creatures have a natural instinct to do certain things, but humans need to be taught almost everything. They need to be taught how to eat, what to eat, how to walk, how to clean themselves, how to brush their teeth. And, when a child reaches five or six years old, he goes to school for the next twelve or fifteen years to learn more.

Just because a baby is born a male does not mean he will grow up and know how to be a man. It's the same with a female child; just because a baby is female doesn't mean she will grow up to become a woman, and know how to be a wife and a mother. Each person has to be taught what it means to be a man or a woman. What does it mean to be a husband or a wife? In today's world everything is based on external factors like how a person looks.

There should be courses in our churches, schools, and universities about *manhood* and *womanhood*, because most people were not taught these things. Society just expects us to know it all.

There is so much confusion out there. A man is not sure if he is a man, and a woman is not sure if she is a woman. Men are trying to become women and women are trying to be men. They are trying to

CHAPTER 7 | THE CHARACTER AND NATURE OF A KING

define who they are. Most of the knowledge we inherit is from the entertainment world—which is far from any reality.

There is a growing generation in our world today that does not want to be identified as male or female. They might have a particular sexual organ, but they don't know what it means to be a man or woman. They are confused because no one taught them about it while they were growing up.

The only thing they were taught is how to have fun. Many of them grew up without both parents at home. Today in our culture, instead of teaching and training our children to be kings and queens, we focus on training them in the things of this world.

Instead of teaching our children the most valuable things about life and godliness, they have been trained to follow the notions of their body and to gratify the lust of their flesh, without ever being accountable for the consequences of their actions.

This is why the Bible says woe to a land when their king is a child. What does this mean? What does a child like to do? A child likes to play and have fun. It also refers to a king who is not mature. Unfortunately, many kings these days sacrifice their purpose and dominion for the sake of having fun:.

> *Woe to you, O land, when your king is a child, and your princes feast in the morning!* –Ecclesiastes 10:16.

A king should not love pleasure:

> *A ruler who lacks understanding is a great oppressor, but he who hates covetousness will prolong his days* –Proverbs 28:16.

A king should hate covetousness. We need to be taught how to be kings in our generation.

The prosperity teaching deceived the saints about their purpose because it focused so much on money; and while we were all busy trying to make money, the devil came in through the back door and stole the nation from us.

How to Respect and Honor a King

Below are some principles the Lord taught me from the book of Esther about the character and nature of a king. Even though King Ahasuerus was a heathen, he was righteous and kind. There is much we can learn from him about being a king.

> Never come stinking into the presence of a king! Remember, they prepared Esther for six months with perfumes. Smell and appearances are important to a king.
>
> When a king asks you to do something, never say *no* or make excuses. If he is a real king, he will hate that. Remember Vasthi the queen.
>
> When you tell a King you are going to do something, the harder or more sacrifice it takes you to do it, the more favor and love the king will feel toward you.
>
> Keeping words and promises are very important to a king. They don't bluff with their mouth and say things they don't mean. They always mean what they say.
>
> Once you have the favor of the king, he will never withhold anything from you, even up to half of his kingdom.
>
> When a king asks you to do something, he is fully aware that you are totally capable of doing it, otherwise he wouldn't ask you.
>
> You need to be respectful, but never shy in front of a king. They don't like shyness, but they love respect.

CHAPTER 7 | THE CHARACTER AND NATURE OF A KING

Kings are usually very generous. They like to bless others, so don't be ashamed to receive something from a king. They do it because that's their nature. Not for any other reason.

Kings like order and beauty. If you read the first chapter of Esther you can see that. Never be clumsy before a king.

Kings like affection and romance. That is why they give such importance to their queen.

When it comes to business, they are very serious. They sign a document or a decree, and it's done.

Kings love music and arts, and anything with quality and excellence. That's why they have musicians and dancers and other professional artists in their palace all the time.

Kings like to have fun, but not all the time. Notice the feast he prepared was for a particular period of time. You have to know when he is happy.

A king likes to show off his queen to others. Don't be shy or rebellious, he hates that. A queen's dress and apparel are very important because it shows the world how pretty she is.

A king likes your *yes* to be yes and your *no* to be no; not maybe. They don't talk like that.

You need to be willing to take orders to be with a king, not because he is mean or unloving, but because it is his nature.

Food is very important to a king. He cares very much about what he eats and likes. He doesn't eat everything. That's why great preparation takes place in cooking for a king.

Romance and sex is very important to a king. He doesn't sleep with just anyone. That's why sometimes it is the most unlikely who steals his heart, someone who is the most beautiful to him.

Kings like to show off their kingdom and wealth to others.

Kings like to honor others and promote them when they do something honorable.

Kings like to record events and great sayings.

Kings listen to the advice of others, if it comes from a reliable source. That's why they have ministers with them in their palace, to ask them when needed. Receiving counsel is not a weakness.

Kings like creativity. Ahasuerus's golden cups were all different in design.

Kings like adventures, trying out new things, and going into new territories.

Once the king is angry, you don't want to be around him.

Kings like to make alliances with other kings and kingdoms.

Kings will not stand for injustice and lying. They abhor those with all their heart.

Honesty and truth are the foundation of a kingdom.

A king would rather kill himself than be killed by his enemy's hand.

They like parties and feasts.

Nothing displeases the king more than saying you are going to do something, and not doing it.

White, blue, purple, silver, gold, and maroon are a king's favorite colors.

Every king has a throne; he needs a private place of his own.

A king has a territory, a place to express his creativity and freedom.

Out of all these, *respecting* and *honoring* them, are the most important.

This teaching is the third part of a series called *Kingdom Awareness Series: Kingdom Secrets to restoring Nations back to God*. I would encourage you to get other materials to read and study. The most important is the book, *The Power and Authority of the Church, Equipping the saints to administer God's kingdom on earth*. You can order these at www.TheKingdomNetwork.org

Restoring and Rebuilding Nations

We have been trying to *reach* nations for far too long. Time has come not just to reach nations but to *rebuild* them. Jesus gave us His kingdom not to just to preach the good news but to rebuild nations as well. It is impossible to peach the gospel of the kingdom and not rebuild nations. It is kings whom God uses to rebuild nations.

If we apply the principles revealed in these books and materials we can win any nation back to God within ten to fifteen years of time, and without a single crusade. That's the challenge God gave me when He inspired me to write these materials.

God has given us another window of opportunity in the United States for the next four years to catch ahold of His vision and plan for His church, or else miss it one more time. He extended His mercy toward us, and I pray that every believer in this nation will recognize this and make use of it.

I believe this teaching has blessed you. I know this is not a complete training manual for training kings and queens, however, it is something to begin with. Please make sure you get Parts 1 & 2 of the *Kingdom Awareness Series,* and study them as well. May the Lord, the great King, open the eyes of our understanding to know more about His kingdom and how it operates.

Prayer

Dear Heavenly Father,

> Thank You so much for giving me Your kingdom, and for creating me as a king on this earth.
>
> Open my eyes to see and receive the mysteries of Your kingdom. Please make me part of what You are doing on this earth right now.
>
> I dedicate my life and everything I have to establishing Your kingdom and for your purpose, to see Your will be done on earth as it is in heaven.

In Jesus Christ's holy name I pray, amen.

Where Do We Go from Here and What Do We Do with This Revelation?

After you read this book you will wonder what you should do with the information you just learned. How will you apply it?

There are many ways you can put these principles to work. The following are a few of these:

- Invite your friends and fellow believers and start a study group using this manual.

- Buy as many copies as you can, and give them to your family and friends.

- Make a curriculum to train children and youth in order to create a king or queen mindset in them before it is formed by their culture and secular media.

- Use the curriculum we have developed for children in Sunday school, church, youth groups, and most importantly at home; to train them on their identity as kings, their purpose, and kingdom assignment.

- Teach our youth about their purpose, instead of instilling in them the spirit of Babylon that likes to have fun all the time.

- Do anything and everything you can to raise up a new generation that God can use to restore our nation to Him.

More Books & Resources

DISCIPLING NATIONS SERIES

Kingdom Mandate (for any donation)

Discovering the Lost Kingdom (Volume 1) $14.00

Purpose, Calling, and Gifts (Volume 2) $15.00

God's Original Design (Volume 3) $20.00

Seeing, Entering, and Manifesting the Kingdom of God (Volume 4) $20.00

The Ekklesia (Volume 5) $30.00

The Gospel of the Kingdom (Volume 6) $20.00

Power and Authority of the Church (Volume 7) $15.00

Kingdom Family (Volume 8) $15.00

The Birthing of a Kingdom Nation (Volume 9) $20.00

What Happened to God? (Volume 10) $20.00

7 Dimensions and Operations of the Kingdom of God (Volume 11) $15.00

Kingdom Economy (Volume 12) $15.00

Kingdom Government (Volume 13) $15.00

Releasing Kings and Queens into God's Original Intent (Volume 14) $10.00

Kingdom Secrets to Restoring Nations Back to God (Volume 15) $20.00

Keys to Fulfilling Your Kingdom Assignment (Volume 16) $15.00

KINGDOM LIVING SERIES

The Three Most Important Decisions of Your Life $15.00

Recognizing God's Timing for Your Life $12.00

Overcoming the Spirit of Poverty $10.00

Seven Kinds of Believers $10.00

7 Dimensions of God's Glory $5.00

7 Dimensions of God's Grace $10.00

7 Kinds of Faith $7.00

HEALING OF THE NATIONS SERIES

Principles of Self Governance $20.00

Kingdom Books for Kids

Genesis 126 Three Volume Book set for boys $25.00

Genesis 126 Three Volume Book set for boys $25.00

Genesis 126 Coloring Books for Boys $15.00

Genesis 126 Coloring Books for Girls $15.00

GENESIS 126 TEACHER'S MANUAL

Level 1 6-8 years $15.00

Level 2 8-10 years $15.00

Level 3 10-12 years $15.00

TO PLACE AN ORDER:

www.TheKingdomNetwork.org
Phone: 1-800-558-5020
Email: info@TheKingdomNetwork.org

Are you struggling to discover your **PURPOSE ?**
You are not supposed to fit in but stand out !

Sign up today for the FREE Online Kingdom Course

DISCOVERING THE LOST KINGDOM

In this course you'll DISCOVER:

>> Your true identity and purpose
>> What God is doing on the earth and how you can partner with Him in it
>> Why God created the earth and put us on this planet
>> And much more ...

Why are people becoming more and more disinterested in **church and religion** globally?
Join the course, and discover
what your soul has been searching for all along.

FREE BOOK AND STUDY GUIDE

Other courses available
>> DISCOVERING PURPOSE, CALLING AND GIFTS
>> SEEING, ENTERING AND MANIFESTING THE KINGDOM
>> GOD'S ORIGINAL DESIGN
>> The Ekklesia
>> The Next move of GOD
   And more ...

Register Now @ www.TheKingdomUniversity.org

Welcome to
KINGDOM DELIVERANCE
— WORKSHOP —

Are you tired of waiting and looking for breakthroughs? Kingdom of God has the answer.

This kingdom deconstruct workshop is divided into EIGHT major categories which deal with the seven major areas of our life. Each one is connected to the next, and so if one of these areas dysfunctions, it will affect all other areas of your life.

1. Relationship with the Father
2. Spiritual Healing
3. Emotional Healing
4. Purpose and Calling
5. Mastering Gifts and Skills
6. Finances—Learning to Live in Kingdom Economy
7. Healing Relationships
8. Physical Health

Take action now. Order all 8 workshop manuals today !

Thank you so much for taking the courses from The Kingdom University. Taking a course is only the first step. We are pleased to present you with the next step—that of going through the process to get rid of all the extra weights that have been slowing and hindering you from fully living out your kingdom assignment.

Call 1 800 558 5020   www.TheKingdomNetwork.org

www.ingramcontent.com/pod-product-compliance
Lightning Source LLC
Chambersburg PA
CBHW070149080526
44586CB00015B/1911